KU-461-345

Reflecting the Word

An Exploration of the Sunday Themes of the ASB Lectionary

First published in Great Britain in 1989 by
KEVIN MAYHEW LTD
Rattlesden
Bury St Edmunds,
Suffolk, IP30 0SZ

©Copyright 1989 by Kevin Mayhew Ltd

Except for brief quotations embodied in critical articles and reviews, this book may not be reproduced in whole or part by any means whatever without the prior written permission of the publisher.

ISBN 0 86209 116 0

Cover design by Graham Johnstone
Typesetting by Typestylers, Ipswich, Suffolk
Printed by J.B. Offset (Marks Tey) Ltd., Marks Tey, Essex

Contents

Foreword		5
About the Contributors		7
9th Sunday before Christmas	Jeremy Davies	9
8th Sunday before Christmas	Paul Oestreicher	11
7th Sunday before Christmas	Richard Holloway	13
6th Sunday before Christmas	Paul Oestreicher	15
5th Sunday before Christmas	Michael Sadgrove	17
1st Sunday in Advent	Richard Holloway	19
2nd Sunday in Advent	Donald Reeves	21
3rd Sunday in Advent	Jeremy Davies	23
4th Sunday in Advent	Jeremy Davies	26
Christmas Day	Richard Holloway	28
1st Sunday after Christmas	Gordon Roe	31
2nd Sunday after Christmas	Robert Williamson	33
The Epiphany of our Lord	Donald Reeves	35
1st Sunday after Epiphany	Richard Holloway	37
2nd Sunday after Epiphany	Donald Reeves	39
3rd Sunday after Epiphany	Michael Sadgrove	41
4th Sunday after Epiphany	Paul Oestreicher	43
5th Sunday after Epiphany	Neville Clark	45
6th Sunday after Epiphany	Gordon Mursell	47
9th Sunday before Easter	Peter Firth	49
8th Sunday before Easter	Peter Firth	51
7th Sunday before Easter	Peter Firth	53
Ash Wednesday	Rodney Matthews	55
1st Sunday in Lent	Neville Clark	57
2nd Sunday in Lent	Neville Clark	59
3rd Sunday in Lent	Gordon Mursell	61
4th Sunday in Lent	Robert Williamson	63
5th Sunday in Lent	Michael Townsend	65
Palm Sunday	Gordon Roe	67

Easter Day	George Carey	69
1st Sunday after Easter	Paul Iles	71
2nd Sunday after Easter	Paul Iles	75
3rd Sunday after Easter	Paul Iles	79
4th Sunday after Easter	Paul Iles	83
5th Sunday after Easter	Neville Clarke	87
Sunday after the Ascension	Gordon Mursell	89
Pentecost Sunday	Perpetua Towell OSB	91
Trinity Sunday	Andrew Naylor	93
2nd Sunday after Pentecost	Perpetua Towell OSB	95
3rd Sunday after Pentecost	Timothy Jenkins	97
4th Sunday after Pentecost	Rodney Matthews	99
5th Sunday after Pentecost	Robert Williamson	101
6th Sunday after Pentecost	Timothy Jenkins	103
7th Sunday after Pentecost	Gordon Roe	105
8th Sunday after Pentecost	Michael Townsend	107
9th Sunday after Pentecost	Neville Clark	109
10th Sunday after Pentecost	Gordon Mursell	111
11th Sunday after Pentecost	John Cole	113
12th Sunday after Pentecost	Peter Hall	115
13th Sunday after Pentecost	Robert Williamson	118
14th Sunday after Pentecost	Rodney Matthews	120
15th Sunday after Pentecost	Neville Clark	122
16th Sunday after Pentecost	John Cole	124
17th Sunday after Pentecost	Rodney Matthews	126
18th Sunday after Pentecost	Peter Hall	128
19th Sunday after Pentecost	Timothy Jenkins	131
20th Sunday after Pentecost	John Cole	133
21st Sunday after Pentecost	John Cole	135
22nd Sunday after Pentecost	Neville Clark	137
Last Sunday after Pentecost	Gordon Roe	139
All Saints Day	Neville Clark	141

Foreword

Since its appearance in 1967, the Joint Liturgical Group Lectionary has provided a stable pattern for reading the scriptures in public worship in many of the major Christian denominations. After initial experimental use, it was incorporated into the *Methodist Service Book* in 1975; the *Church of Scotland Service Book* in 1979; after slight modification, it was incorporated into the *Alternative Service Book* of the Church of England in 1980; and it is widely used by the Baptist Churches and the United Reformed Church. The reflections in this book, based on the themes and readings of every Sunday and other Holy Days, are designed to accompany the Lectionary, and have been written by a group of diverse people who represent the various denominations who use it.

The reflections may be used in various ways. They may serve as outlines for the preacher, and some will make useful additional 'readings' at the Eucharist or Office. They will also prove to be invaluable for those who are looking for material for personal reflection, or corporate discussion, based on the themes of Sunday worship.

If one thing characterises these reflections, it is that they all encourage the reader to think *theologically* about the meaning and message of the scriptures. This doesn't mean that they are full of high-flying jargon! It means that each author is sharing with us the joys and sorrows, and the confidences and uncertainties that are part and parcel of any Christian pilgrimage. Put simply, theology often means trying to see where God, and his message in the scriptures, fits into our experience of life and our plans for the future. And those using this book will find much to encourage a broader vision of faith and life.

However, one sad fact remains in that only one woman accepted an invitation to contribute to this book, despite invitations being made to equal numbers of men and women. While this may open all sorts of questions, it must still remind us that any vision of the Kingdom of God is inadequate unless it incorporates the physical, spiritual and emotional experience of the whole of humanity.

We offer this book, therefore, in the hope that it will be a helpful guide for all who meet as a community of faith, to seek the presence of the risen Lord, and his coming to us in word and sacrament.

About the Contributors

GEORGE CAREY Is Bishop of Bath and Wells.

NEVILLE CLARK Is Principal of the South Wales Baptist College, and Dean of the Faculty of Theology at the University of Wales College, Cardiff. He is a member of the Joint Liturgical Group, and is widely recognised as a leading scriptural scholar.

JOHN COLE Is the St. Hugh's Missioner for South Humberside in the Diocese of Lincoln.

JEREMY DAVIES Is Precentor of Salisbury Cathedral. He has been a Chaplain at university colleges in London and Cardiff, and also an Editor of *Christian*.

PETER FIRTH Is Bishop of Malmesbury.

PETER HALL Is Bishop of Woolwich.

RICHARD HOLLOWAY Is Bishop of Edinburgh. He is also widely known as a writer and broadcaster.

PAUL ILES Is Precentor of Hereford Cathedral.

TIMOTHY JENKINS Is Chaplain at the University of Nottingham.

RODNEY MATTHEWS Is Minister of Llanthewy Road Baptist Church, Newport, Gwent. He is also widely involved with the various ecumenical bodies in Wales.

GORDON MURSELL Is Chaplain and Tutor in Spirituality at Salisbury and Wells Theological College.

ANDREW NAYLOR Is a member of the Community of St Peter.

PAUL OESTREICHER Is Director of International Ministry at Coventry Cathedral.

DONALD REEVES Is Rector of St James's, Piccadilly, London. He is also well known as a writer and broadcaster.

GORDON ROE Is Bishop of Huntingdon.

MICHAEL SADGROVE Is Precentor of Coventry Cathedral.

PERPETUA TOWELL OSB Is Abbess of the Benedictine Community at West Malling, Kent.

MICHAEL TOWNSEND Is a Minister in the Huddersfield Pennine Methodist Circuit.

ROBERT WILLIAMSON Is Bishop of Bradford.

Ninth Sunday
before Christmas

〜

The Creation

Jeremy Davies

*'There are 364 days when you might get unbirthday presents.'
'Certainly,' said Alice, 'and only one for birthday presents you
know. There's glory for you!' 'I don't know what you mean by
glory', Alice said. Humpty Dumpty smiled contemptuously, 'Of
course you don't until I tell you. I meant there's a nice knock-
down argument for you!' 'But glory doesn't mean a nice knock-
down argument', Alice objected. 'When I use a word,' Humpty
Dumpty said in rather a scornful tone, 'It means just what I choose
it to mean — neither more nor less.'*

YOU could say that 'glory' is so much part of our religious
jargon, as commonplace as 'amen' at the end of our prayers,
that we rather take it for granted; make it mean what we choose
it to mean. And often we don't recognise just how rich and
paradoxical a word it is for Christian belief. Glory at one level
has all the features of triumphalism — of power and might and
splendour. Republicans in America discovered that 'glory' went
well with 'alleluia', both to express the majesty of God and the
aspirations of the Republican cause, and so *Glory, Glory, Alleluia*
became the Battle Hymn of the Republic. But nothing could be
more glorious, in this sense, than the description of the creation
of the world which we find in the two creation narratives of the
first chapters of Genesis. In those stories God, simply by saying
'Let there be', brought order out of chaos, caused light to shine,
waters to swell, living beings to creep, crawl, fly, swim and walk
upright in the likeness of God himself. Here is a picture of an
all powerful, all knowing, controlling genius who fashions and
moulds and commands. There's glory for you.

But God's work in creation is not complete; for this is not a
static, inorganic, monolithic construction. On the contrary, God's
greatest creative risk was the sharing of God-likeness and creative

9

power with his creatures. Such power-sharing suggests that creation is in process of becoming. The biblical understanding of how that power-sharing developed is contained in the succeeding chapters of Genesis which tell of human fall from grace through disobedience. And the saga continues with God renewing his covenant with humankind and men and women continually breaking their side of the bargain. The glory of the former days is lost, never to be recaptured (and barely even glimpsed by men and women), whose sense of glory of God is overlaid by the idol of their own transient glory.

That is until a new re-creative enterprise was taken in hand by God. Or rather, not a *new* creation, for this divine initiative had all the hallmarks of the original seven-day wonder. God's new initiative was again risk-taking; again marked by overflowing love towards the creation; again demanded that the creator should spend himself to the uttermost. But there *was* something new about it, all the same. Whereas in the beginning God spoke and it was done; whereas in the beginning God's word had moulded, fashioned and brought into being, now that same Word was itself subject, fashioned and moulded, dependent on the love, goodwill and generosity of the created order. God's Word, — enfleshed in Jesus — was put at risk, as the only way God knew of 'getting his own back'; a way which seemed to put aside glory in order that God's heart should be known to be beating in time with the human heart.

'There's glory for you.'

Eighth Sunday
before Christmas

The Fall

Paul Oestreicher

WITHOUT a deep sense of mystery, the Christian faith can easily become a set of theological propositions which will, when that faith is put to the test, satisfy neither heart nor mind. 'There are many things you cannot understand now,' Jesus said to his disciples. That is no less true of this generation. At no point is this more true than when we are confronted with evil, evil within us and evil around us. We have no rational explanation for what has gone wrong. And the closer we are to God, the more keenly are we aware of how wrong things have gone, how alienated we are from what we should be. Those whom others call saints have been most aware of their own sin and of their need for forgiveness.

The Jewish and the Christian dream, and all human striving for perfection, is a deep-seated need to regain paradise. The dream is rooted in the conviction that there is divine goodness at the heart of creation and that it is not beyond our ultimate reach. To diagnose the disease is relatively easy. The powerful symbolism of our expulsion from paradise as a result of human disobedience and the subsequent death-feud between Cain and Abel are graphic descriptions of what the human race is like. Present in these myths (no, myths are *not* fairy tales but attempts to express the almost inexpressible) is the assumption that we have the God-given gift to make choices between good and evil, between life and death.

But at no point can we explain the source of sin. The invention of a personal devil or the recognition of a mysterious evil power in the universe raises as many questions as it answers. If all things have their source in God, then — however we define the Fall — God, at the very least, has allowed it to happen. Sydney Carter's: " 'It's God they ought to crucify, instead of you and me,' I said to the carpenter, a' 'hanging on the tree' " is a cry from the human heart that is wholly valid. In the century of Auschwitz and Hiroshima (and the list could go on and on and on . . .) any denial of our perversity, any claim that, in the last resort, all is well itself seems to provide more evidence of that perversity.

Hell is a perfectly proper way of describing the conditions in which many people live. It may be a very private hell or a very public one. It is certainly so terrible for countless people and so deeply destructive of life on our planet that no dogmatic statement alone can put things to rights. Such 'cheap grace' is not on offer. Beware of those Christians who appear to be offering it. Beware of religion with the perpetual smile. It is counterfeit!

What then of 'faith, hope and love'? Just so much false comfort? The question needs to be asked. And then the mystery affirmed that faith, hope and love are as real as fear, despair and hatred. Good and evil are locked in a cosmic struggle that is present in every human being. Personally and socially our potentially divine humanity is challenged to defeat evil with goodness.

At the heart of the mystery is the experience that God in Christ, God in the divine humanity of Jesus of Nazareth, does not leave us alone in the struggle but totally shares the pain of life and the pain of death, death at its most perverse. Love, rewarded with rejection, scorn and execution. And love's response: 'Father forgive'. There is no humiliation, no degradation that God himself does not share. And from the depths of undeserved suffering comes the assurance of unlimited compassion.

The closest we can approach to the mystery is to recognise God suffering in every tortured person and God suffering too in the person of the torturer: taking sin and its cost on himself. God, loving, unconditionally and expecting us to share that love with others: 'If a rich person sees his neighbour in need and fails to share his wealth ('closes his heart') how can he claim that he loves God?'

Seventh Sunday
before Christmas

The Election of God's People: Abraham

Richard Holloway

ABRAHAM is always thought of as the great exemplar or archetype of faith, but there is shadow as well as light in his story, terror as well as consolation in his encounter with God. The image we all like is that of Abraham the pilgrim, the wayfarer, the man who went out at God's command, 'not knowing where he was to go', as the Letter to the Hebrews puts it. This image certainly appeals to us today. We talk about the Church as a pilgrimage and we think of faith as a characteristic that keeps us on the move, refusing to let us settle down or sink back into ease or possession. Like Abraham, we are looking for a country we do not yet possess, we are searching for a kingdom we can see only from afar, so we keep moving, we are nomads upon the face of the earth, always setting our face to what lies ahead. This aspect of the story of Abraham is rich with food for thought and meditation. It warns us against the diseases that afflict the settled community: defensiveness, moral cowardice, the making of idols, especially theological idols, the love of comfort and peace at whatever price, and a profound suspicion of change. Against all this we must place the image of Abraham folding up his tents and moving out and moving on, 'not knowing where he was to go', but knowing that God was ahead, out there in the wilderness that purified, the wilderness that tempted and tested and refined the soul.

And this is where we are led by Abraham, into the shadow, into the darkness of God. As well as the picture of Abraham the wanderer upon the face of the earth, up there on his horse or his camel, a proud Bedouin, traversing the desert, we must also face the picture of Abraham poised above his son Isaac, knife in hand, ready to plunge it into his heart at the command of God. What are we to make of this image in an age that recognises the sacredness of children, yet all too often sees them used as pawns

13

in the games their parents play or used as objects for adult lust or cruelty? Traditionally, this image of Abraham's sacrifice of his son Isaac is seen as a metaphor of radical faith. God's promise to Abraham was that in Isaac and his seed would his name be blessed, yet here he is being called upon by God to sacrifice the very ground on which the promise was based. Radical faith, we are told, abandons everything to God. It calls us at times to acts of heroic absurdity. Nothing is God but God and at any time we may be called by God to surrender even those things which God has given us, those things through which God has come to us and maybe even the people closest to us, the ones whose names are graved upon our hands. We can really get going on this theme and preachers often do. There is something about the heroic absurdity of it all that captures faith in all its paradox. But we must not forget that we have conveniently transposed the sacrifice of Isaac from a murder into a metaphor, but a murder it would have been. And maybe this is exactly where the real greatness of Abraham can be discerned.

If we look at the story of Abraham and Isaac in historical terms, we have to conclude that we are catching a glimpse of the most horrific form of religion in history — human sacrifice. Where God is conceived of as a devouring monster demanding to be fed with human blood, we confront the grisly reality of human sacrifice. Biblical religion is, on one level, the story of an evolution in the human understanding of God; and in the story of Abraham and Isaac we could be at one of its major points of development. The man Abraham, called upon to sacrifice his son in the name of a cruel God, rebels in the name of the God of mercy: 'I require mercy and not sacrifice,' God tells us later in the Old Testament, but was it through Abraham that the original insight came? There has always been development in religion, as the nature of God is gradually and fitfully disclosed to us, but it takes faith to discern the new truth we are being led to. Sometimes we are called upon by God to abandon the things we once believed, in order to see more clearly the one in whom alone we are to trust. There is the faith that trusts and there is the faith that rebels, and Abraham is the great exemplar of both.

Sixth Sunday
before Christmas

*The Promise of
Redemption: Moses*
Paul Oestreicher

REDEMPTION is one of those safe religious words that trips off the tongue of the preacher and flows unobtrusively in one ear and out the other of the religious consumer. It does not, generally, pass through the mind. No disturbance is caused. It is part of a whole insiders' vocabulary. The programmed Christian expects to be fed these words, feels well satisfied and has every reason to believe that what she or he has been fed is the Word of God itself.

To the 'unconverted' these words convey no meaning at all. Shouting them from the roof-tops is no way of breaking through the communication barrier. Nor will packaging them in ancient or modern hymn tunes do the trick. The breakthrough to a living faith does not just call for a new vocabulary, it calls for something like re-birth, with all the attendant traumas. At least to begin with, we cannot do without words, words that begin to open the mind and strengthen the heart. Liberation is such a word. Prisoners know what it means. Slaves know what it means. For hungry people it means bread.

Liberation can, of course, be forced back into a religious ghetto, narrowed down to fit into a set of doctrines. It can be tamed. But not easily and not at all if, as the scriptures insist, our faith is about discipleship. And discipleship (another word in need of a fresh-airing) is about following a person; following, not blindly, but out of a trusting relationship.

Moses was such a person. He was close to God. The people of Israel, in slavery in Egypt, saw that he was close to God. When Moses gave his people God's law to live by, they knew that it was genuine, even when they failed to observe it. Now they could measure their own lives against the demands of a just and caring God. 'Trust me,' said Moses, 'and — against all the odds — I shall lead you to the borders of the promised land; lead you out of slavery.'

Moses was true to his word. And God kept faith with Moses. Then the people of Israel began a new, long wait for the promised Messiah who would usher in 'a new heaven and a new earth'. Could the young, radical rabbi, Jesus of Nazareth, possibly be that person? Again, against all the odds, some of his fellow Jews believed it and followed him. Only four, it seems, had the kind of faith, however, to follow him all the way to the place of his execution for the crime of blasphemy and of allegedly claiming to be some kind of king. Of those four, three were women. (So much for the male fantasy of the 'weaker sex'!) One of those women was to be the first to tell the world that Jesus was alive. Alive to give new hope to all people: men and women and children, Jews and Samaritans and Romans, friends and enemies. Now the mosaic law, like all good gifts not to be despised, was no longer the last word. The last word was love. That was true freedom. And always had been. 'Love God and love one another' had always been the summary of the old law. Jesus spelt out what that meant by how he lived and died: no one would or could be excluded from God's love. This was not cheap grace that could be earned with a little effort. It was a free gift, inviting love in response.

But Jesus warned his friends that their new found freedom was dangerous in a world of sin. They were to expect treatment no better than his own: 'All will hate you for your allegiance to me, but those who hold out to the end will be saved.' That is the good news that will wipe away our easy smiles and, in the end, all our tears. Then words like liberation and redemption will be needed no more.

Fifth Sunday before Christmas

The Remnant of Israel

Michael Sadgrove

THE idea of the remnant is an ambiguous one. On the one hand, it stands for faith and commitment bravely adhered to against all the odds. The remnant is that community, usually small in number, in which the traditions of worship and response to God have been cherished, and remain alive and compelling, even in situations of persecution and apostasy. That is clearly the intention behind today's choice of theme: to recall that Christian obedience has its price, that it will often be the choice only of the few, and that it calls for perseverance in the face of a dismissive or hostile world. But the other side of the remnant idea is less appealing: the tendency of most 'remnants' in religious or political life to think that they, and they alone, remain 'true', 'orthodox', 'faithful' to the particular vision or insight whose name they bear. The Bible bears witness to how easily this ugly stream of self-righteous complacency could sour the life of both Old and New Testament communities.

The word 'remnant' is introduced in the Old Testament lesson in the Eucharist for Year 2 (Isaiah 10:20-23). Here, the remnant is associated with the promise that the people will return to God, though whether many or few is rather obscurely left unclear. For Isaiah the prophet, the salvation of the surviving remnant was a key idea (his son was named *Shear Jashub*, 'A Remnant will return', Isaiah 7:3). The story of Elijah, in the Year 1 Old Testament lesson (1 Kings 19:9-18), is perhaps a warning against moving too quickly into a 'remnant' view of things. Elijah, believing himself to be the only surviving Israelite faithful to the covenant with Yahweh, has to be told that there are indeed several thousand *others* who have not succumbed to the worship of the Phoenician God Baal-Melqart.

Both New Testament readings at the Eucharist are taken from Romans 9-11, the section in Paul's letter in which he deals with

Israel's election and the salvation of the gentiles in the divine plan. These three chapters are often relegated to the status of a parenthesis in Romans, as if they were not really relevant to Paul's developing argument. In fact, they are crucial to it, for it is only by establishing that God is Lord of human history that Paul's claim that, in Christ, *all* are made alive, can be believed. The Year 2 reading (Romans 9:19-28), quoting the Isaiah passage, celebrates the inclusion of gentiles into the covenant people of God; while in Year 1 (Romans 11:13-24), their inclusion is likened to the grafting-on of a new growth upon the original tree. Both passages need to be read against the background of Romans 8:28-end, and as looking forward to the joyous conclusion of Romans 11:33-end. The faithfulness of the remnant leads finally to a salvation that is universal.

The gospel readings both derive from essentially the same source: Jesus' teaching about the last things (Matthew 24:37-44, Mark 13:14-23). These passages bring us very close to that imminent end-of-world expectation that was characteristic of Jesus' time. Using conventional Old Testament images, Jesus speaks of the coming tribulations as the necessary birth-pangs to the new age of the kingdom. The summons, in both passages, is to persevering faith, and watchfulness for the signs of the Son of Man's coming. The key to this idea, common throughout the apocalyptic writings of the time, is to be found in the Lord's Prayer: 'Do not bring us to the test (or time of trial), but deliver us from evil.' The 'remnant' are those who have come safely through the testing time that precedes the kingdom, and are thus ready to enter into the fulness of God's reign.

Perhaps no Sunday of the year has been allocated more difficult readings than this one. The language and imagery of all but the Elijah passage can seem strikingly out of tune with the more congenial requirements of most worshippers today. But readings like these remind us that the biblical text is a rugged thing, with demand as well as comfort, challenge as well as encouragement. The picture of the remnant leaves us in no doubt as to what Bonhoeffer called 'the cost of discipleship'.

First Sunday
in Advent

The Advent Hope

Richard Holloway

ONE of the intriguing things about modern society is the persistence of superstition in various forms. Astrology is intensely popular and even those of us who may be a bit sceptical about it sneak a look at our own horoscopes in magazine and newspaper. Down the centuries men and women have sought knowledge of the future by various devices. There is, for instance, the famous crystal ball, greatly favoured by fairground gypsies; the ancient art of haruspication that tried to discover the outline of the future by poking about in the entrails of chickens; and in the street I grew up in there were several old women who had perfected the ancient art of reading tea leaves. The craze for fortune telling got so bad at one time that the Church tried to ban it, a good example of how often the Church wastes its energies trying to condemn things it would be better trying to understand. But why is there this great interest in fortune telling or future gazing? There seem to be two main reasons for it.

First of all, we experience a fundamental uncertainty and anxiety as we face the future. Who knows what might befall us? Our present happiness or contentment is a very slender thread which can be broken in an instant. A tiny blood vessel bursts in the brain of someone we love dearly, and the thread is broken. A driver has one drink too many and a young life we adore is destroyed on some grim roadway, and the thread is broken. Someone we thought to be true and steadfast turns from us and changes joy into misery, and the thread is broken. These things happen every day to people we know. They can happen to us. So we are faced with a fundamental anxiety as we gaze towards the future. If we are not careful, the uncertainty can lead to a morbid anxiety that can destroy our ability to enjoy the present. The future threatens us.

But along with this uncertainty or anxiety about the future goes a fundamental need in us to look forward with hope. We all need something to look forward to, some joy that lies ahead, some promised fulfilment. There is something in us that disposes us to look ahead. Think of the amount of time we spend planning for the future. This is especially true of children, but it characterises adults as well, which is why many of us carry those big, fat diaries and planners around with us and constantly check what is coming next. We are endlessly looking forward: to Christmas, to the holidays, to our next promotion, to the new movie at the local *ABC* or the new novel from our favourite novelist. In the language of the cinema, we are all eager for forthcoming attractions or future presentations. The future is full of promise.

This all adds up to two very special needs in human nature: we want to be secure, free from threat; and we want something to look forward to. So the future tantalises us. It is both promise and threat. What will it bring? Will it be the oil of gladness or the ashes of mourning, the garland of praise or the spirit of heaviness, as Isaiah puts it? Will we be set at the King's right hand or at his left?

The nature and quality of the future is, of course, one of the great themes of Advent. It calls us to look forward to the future in hope and not to waste our energies in anxious imaginings, but it wants us to base our confidence in the future, not on wishful thinking but on hopeful and purposive acting. We are warned that, uncertain as the future is, it does unfold from our own present. We shall be our own judges in that day, because we'll be our own handiwork. Scripture uncompromisingly reminds us that we make our own future — and that it's later than we think!

Second Sunday of Advent

The Word of God in the Old Testament

Donald Reeves

TODAY is Bible Sunday — the day when, as the Collect puts it, we ask God to 'help us so to hear them (holy Scriptures), to read, mark, learn and inwardly digest them that we may embrace and for ever hold fast the hope of everlasting life.'

Those words deliberately echo one of the New Testament readings: there the writers remind us that 'All Scripture is inspired by God and us useful for teaching the truth.' (2 Timothy 3:15)

But how are we to read the Bible? Some say, 'The Bible says ...,' and while they may not interpret the Bible literally, they would certainly say that the Bible is innerrant; it is free from error. How could it be since it is God's inspired Word to us?

Understanding the Bible like this means a lot of energy and guile has to be generated to iron out contradictions and confusions. I once read a commentary which said that Jesus ascended twice into heaven — because the Ascension is mentioned twice, once at the end of Luke's Gospel, and once at the start of Acts!

But any thoughtful reading of the different books written at different times and in different places makes it impossible to read the Bible like this. The innerrant approach raises more questions than it answers; moreover, on some matters the Bible is plainly wrong; for example, its acceptance of slavery, and its attitude to women. And on other matters — like the nuclear threat, or the population explosion, or the North/South divide, it is of little help.

To read the Bible so that it resonates with our own experience requires an act of imagination. It is as if we leave our familiar surroundings, everything that we take for granted, and settle, for a time, in a remote place (where there is another language spoken and where the customs are so different from our own). We stay long enough there — first just as an observer and then as one who participates in the life of this unusual and strange community.

And then we return to our own land — the landscape is, of course, familiar, but our absence highlights much that we have previously ignored or taken for granted; we notice, for example, how strained our faces are in big cities, or how dirty everything is.

To read the Bible requires that sort of willingness to become immersed in that ancient world where men and women recounted the ways God had revealed himself to them; the journey is made backwards to that distant world, and forwards into our own, backwards and forwards. And then slowly it is possible to catch the resonances of God speaking in the midst of all the terrors and turbulence of our own day.

But all the churches are in difficulties with the Bible. There is no clear concensus as to its role. The Bible is the Word of God; it is not about God. It is 'of God'. But every word comes from human beings, and the Bible is thus conditioned by our limitations. Thus scientific, literary, historical and archaeological disciplines are needed to determine what the authors meant when they wrote. This is where the divergences and difficulties begin. For 150 years, scholars have dissected the Bible. We are still not yet in a position where Catholic, Orthodox and Protestant churches — the community of faith — can agree on a framework in which the Bible can be interpreted. Until this happens, the Bible will continue to lose its authority.

Third Sunday
of Advent

༄

The Forerunner

Jeremy Davies

THE season of Advent is an ambivalent season in the Church's calendar — somewhere between feast and fast, — reflecting the fact that until the 13th century the Roman Church celebrated the four weeks of Advent as a celebratory prelude to Christmas, while the Gallic Church kept the five or six weeks of Advent (originally from the feast of St. Martin on November 11th) as a time of penance. The sombre themes of the Last Judgement, the Second Coming of Christ and the four Last Things provided the material for sober Christian reflection. Today our own western celebration of Advent keeps alive this duality: we prepare to celebrate God made flesh in the story of Christmas but there is also a sense of the darkness of our world, of human wilfulness and self-centredness and the impending judgement.

The readings for the Sunday before Advent plunge us into the cosmic drama, a battle between good and evil, with an urgent sense of living at the overlap of the ages — (as the first Christians, whom the writer of Mark's gospel was addressing, must certainly have felt). And the readings for Advent Sunday itself confirm and emphasised the sense of urgency, and the nearness of God's kingdom. But there is also the notion within the Advent theme that God's judgement and his love are almost indistinguishable; two sides of the same transparent coin. At the same time as the cataclysmic drama is being staged, God is working his divine purposes through the most unlikely agencies of revelation, — through the scriptures (the theme for Advent 2); through the ascetic ministry of John the Baptist (Advent 3), and most unlikely of all, through a slip of a girl, Mary (Advent 4). It is as though, while the world was caught up in its process of self-destruction, God yet again trusts his purposes of redemption and transfiguration to frail and feeble human resources — resources liable to be misheard, misquoted, ignored, marginalised and done to death. It is as though, even while we hear the hoofs of the horses of the Apocalypse pounding, God is finding new, though fragile, ways of restoring the face of the earth.

John the Baptist represents an unconditional, uncompromising, prophetic ministry. He is the last of the Old Testament prophets but he is also the Forerunner: he is the end of the old line and the herald of the new. The Collect for the birth of St. John the Baptist (which we celebrate on June 24th) runs like this: 'May we after his example constantly speak the truth, boldly rebuke vice and patiently suffer for the truth's sake.' Certainly men and women who constantly speak the truth and boldly rebuke vice usually suffer for the truth's sake. For though they may influence people (and we are told that many thousands flocked to hear John the Baptist and be baptised by him) they certainly don't make friends among their contemporaries. For the prophet is not one who forsees the future so much as reads the times in which he is living: one who sees with heightened awareness (and often with apocalyptic clarity) the depraved self-destructiveness of society and the religion that colludes with it. Very often such prophets are found, like John the Baptist on the edges of society, uncomfortably reminding the Church and the State and individuals of what God requires: 'What is it that the Lord asks of you? Only to act justly, to love loyalty and to walk wisely before your God.' (Micah 6:8).

D. H. Lawrence in his essay *Chaos in Poetry* describes the poet as 'an enemy of convention' who makes a slit in the umbrella which humankind erects between itself and the everlasting whirl. 'And lo the glimpse of chaos is a vision, a window to the sun; but after a while getting used to the vision and not liking the genuine draught from chaos, commonplace man daubs a simulacrum of the window that opens on to chaos and patches the umbrella with the painted patch of the simulacrum. That is he has got used to the vision, it is part of his house decoration.' What D. H. Lawrence says about the poet we may say about the prophet who similarly opens up the conscience, and consciousness of men and women who are gradually 'going bleached and stifled under their parasol.'

Maybe the Church is called to prophetic witness; this is the view of Kenneth Leech who in his book *The Social God* says: 'the primary task of the Church *vis-à-vis* the world is to confront it and to preach to it ... Today the servant Church is in danger

24

of obscuring and replacing the prophetic Church. Yet for the Bible caring is not enough. Biblical social concern is not simply with helping casualties on the Jericho Road but with the building of a new highway and a new city.' What is certain is that certain individuals within the Church are called to tread that lonely and costly path, of prophetic utterance, trodden before them by John the Baptist, and so to keep alive the sense of God's judgement and his love.

Fourth Sunday of Advent

The Annunciation

Jeremy Davies

FROM my study window I see the bustle of the first day of a university term: propped against the same window is a large postcard — a reproduction of Fra Angelico's Annunciation that adorns the cloisters of the Church of St. Marco in Florence. I look at the mêlée of people with the Annunciation in the corner of my eye. The Virgin sits there — as though she had always sat there — waiting. Fra Angelico conveys her composure and her expectancy. Her left hand moves in welcome, not without apprehension. The angel bearing God's Word nonetheless bends the knee before such wholeness in being. The Virgin is poised and composed to receive God's Word — indeed only such composure can enable her not only to receive but to appropriate and absorb God's Word wholly into her being. To such a degree does the Virgin absorb God's Word that she bears it and gives it life in the world. That picture by Fra Angelico speaks to me of all this as no other of the many hundreds of Renaissance Annunciations can. I look at our assembling students through the perspective of that picture. The response of Mary to the devastating announcement is simply 'so be it'. It is as though her whole life has been a preparation for this moment when the redemption of the world hung on the yea or the nay of a slip of a girl from Galilee.

Jesus subsequently learnt to say 'so be it', 'Amen' from his mother, and he taught this same 'Amen' to his friends. 'When you pray say "Our Father in heaven may your name be hallowed and *your will be done*".' And not being one to preach and not practice, we find him, when up against the most awful odds, knowing that the day would be his last, uttering the same words of acceptance: 'if possible deliver me from this labour but not my will but yours be done.' Amen. So be it. It is this word 'Amen' that characterises the Christian response to God and to life. It is a little word with vast implications because it says yes to God in response to God's incredible yes to men and women. This 'yes' is the heart of Christian prayer; it is the heart of Jesus' own prayer and life. As the Annunciation of God's Word to the Virgin and as Jesus's own response to impending death suggests, saying 'yes' is not a matter of being nice to God or nice to our fellows in an idle moment. Amen involves commitment and faith. It is very different from putting up with, or simply tolerating or turning a blind eye to what life brings. To say Amen is not to be indifferent to events and people; it is not a fatalism which says 'I cannot control what goes on so I will resign myself to it!' Acceptance of life and its ways means a commitment and an engagement, a sense of responsibility as well as awe in the face of life's problems and difficulties. It involves what Alan Ecclestone in his book *Yes to God* describes as passion and engagement. All this is involved in saying 'Amen' because we recognise the passion and engagement that God demonstrates in saying yes to us. Alan Ecclestone puts it this way: 'passion and engagement are brought together in the yes God spoke to the world and our attempted yes of response cannot be otherwise spoken.'

Christmas Day

God With Us

Richard Holloway

IN many ways it is a pity that the phrase 'no room at the inn' has gone into our language and sunk into our consciousness, because it is almost certainly misunderstood by most of us.

In the first place, we probably ought to revise our picture of the inn they came to in Bethlehem. It wasn't a hotel or boarding house as we think of these things, with multi-level parking for camels round the back. A middle-eastern inn was really a square of covered stalls built round an open courtyard. Travellers arrived and booked in for the night on a first-come-first-served basis, the way they do in caravan and parking sites in this country today. If you got there in time you got a stall, a place to camp. The innkeeper supplied feed for your beasts and a fire for you. You brought your own food. The animals were bedded down in the open courtyard in the centre. Latecomers had, perforce, to join the animals. It was, after all, first-come-first-served. And Mary and Joseph got there late. There were many travelling and Mary and Joseph, because of her condition, made time more slowly than most. All the stalls were taken so they, like many others, had to make do with the open courtyard among the animals. Admittedly it was an awful place in which to give birth to a child, but there was no conspiracy, no hard-faced social oppression. It was first-come-first-served, and they were late. Too many others had got to the inn before them.

So it was not intentionally meant, and the innkeeper was probably a decent sort. Nevertheless, it makes you think, doesn't it? Most human beings aren't oppressors, but things have a perplexing way of crowding in on them as they did on that innkeeper, so that tragic things happen and precious opportunities are lost. No one is to blame, of course, and yet ... The story of Christmas is the story of God's coming to us and he always seems to get there too late. As John's Gospel puts it: 'He came to his own home, and his own people received him not'. Why? Why does he never get to Bethlehem on time, ahead of the others? Why is it always too late to admit him?

I think the reason why there is no room left for God is that he is not one of the things that press in on us; he is not one thing among many; he is what gives meaning to everything else. God is the ground of the existence of all things, but his existence does not press in upon us with the same directness or unavoidability as the things he has made. In order to think about God, to think about the meaning of everything, as opposed to reacting to the stimulus of something, we have to stand back a bit from life and make a free choice: we have to stop the assembly line, the endless flow of demand and desire, and ask about the meaning of the whole: 'What does it mean?' It's obviously easy to avoid this question, because all the other things get there first, capture us, own us, obsess us. We are held in this great, inexorable system of one-thing-after-another, and to wrench ourselves out of it even for a moment, to ask what it means, requires an enormous act of courage and will; and most of us prefer to be driven thoughtlessly by the thoughtless rush of life. Anyway, most of us are not really sure we want to find God, recognise God, confront God, for we fear what it might mean and the changes we might have to make. God's presence disturbs us, challenges us, lights up too much we want to keep hidden, even from ourselves. Altogether, then God's much, much safer out there in the courtyard.

That, of course, is where he stays. God's coming to us is always, by his own will, ignorable by us. He comes, always, in a lowly way, a way that's easy to dismiss — in weakness, in poverty, in simplicty, the divine straggler, the man at the end of the line who arrives just as we put up the shutters. He's easy to dismiss, to pretend not to notice, to turn from, to crowd out of our lives: just ignore him and he goes away — or almost, but only *almost,* because the divine stranger never quite goes away. He's always turning up in our lives, standing on the periphery, catching our eyes in spite of ourselves, filling us with a sudden loneliness in the midst of the crowd, stabbing us with a sudden longing to make an end of all pretence and own him Lord. He's always turning up in our lives: a thought catches us at the turning of the stairs; or there's a sudden snatch of a forgotten tune from behind a door that closes too soon; a cross glinting on a steeple is seen from the window of a speeding train; a forgotten confirmation card turns up in an old book; something your mother once said to you is remembered when you're too old to cry; and there is the strange light at the year's end, caught too swiftly on the ice-grey river. It's always too late. 'Late, late, have I loved thee.' He's always late, late getting to Bethlehem, but he keeps on coming, keeps on moving along that road, travelling, travelling towards us to stand mutely at our heart's door.

First Sunday
after Christmas

〜

Sharing His Divinity

Gordon Roe

ONE of the attractions of Christmas is that it assures us of
a God who shares our earthly life. He is born of a woman
in an ordinary earthly family: 'And he feeleth for our sadness and
he shareth in our gladness'. This is a deeply pastoral truth which
helps to make sense of the inequalities and sufferings of life. Ours
is a God who does not remain aloof from his creation, but has
entered it in order to redeem it.

But there is another side of·that truth which has been
emphasised more in the East than in the West. That is, as St.
Irenaeus and other Christian Fathers have said, 'God made himself
man, that man might become God', or as we pray in the collect,
'Grant that, as he came to share in our humanity, so we may share
the life of his divinity.' This prayer reflects the mysterious words
from the Gospel, 'From his fullness have we all received grace
upon grace' (John 1:16), or as we read in the Second Epistle of
Peter, 'He has given us the very great and precious gifts he
promised, so that ... you ... may come to share the divine
nature.' (2 Peter 1:4)

This could all sound overweening and pretentious. Any talk
of man becoming like God seems to smack of the optimism of
the nineteenth century, when man was tempted to believe that
the increase of knowledge gave him a command over nature which
was God-like. Nothing could be further from the mind of the
fourth evangelist or the early Fathers. They were bowled over
by the wonder of God becoming man, and although they perceived
that this truth did throw light on the human condition, for them
it was much more important for what it told them about God:
'the only Son, who is in the bosom of the Father has made him
known.' (John 1:18) Far from encouraging humanity to be too
big for its boots they are trying to bring it back to a sense of awe
and responsibility, simply because, by the incarnation, it has been

drawn into an intimate relationship with God.

A hint of how this is to be understood is found in the passage from Galatians 4:1-7, where the fact that God sent his own son born of a woman is said to mean that we have passed from being slaves to having the status of sons.

A child growing up has a vision of the world of her parents. She sees that they have wisdom and freedoms that she does not have and she looks forward to the day when, as a result of their training, she will have them too. It may be only a vision limited to the power to come in as late as she likes, or the freedom to leave her room untidy. But through such limited perceptions she is drawn into a life of greater reality and maturity. We, who have been told that unless we become as little children we cannot enter the Kingdom of Heaven, also have terribly limited perceptions, but because of the incarnation and all that follows from it, we are being drawn (unless we stubbornly resist) into a life of greater reality, God himself.

Second Sunday after Christmas

∽

The Holy Family

Robert Williamson

FOR many people the term 'Holy Family' conjures up an idyllic picture of what family life should be. One of the Collects for today, with its careful stress on love and obedience, can suggest that all was sweetness and light within that little family at Nazareth. Though we know that there was another side to the story. Like every other earthly family there were times of stress and strain, there were experiences of misunderstanding and heartache and, if we take one of today's gospels (Luke 2:41-end) at its face value, a fair amount of aggrieved straight talking!

Some of us, if not all of us, might well heave a sigh of relief at that fact, for idyllic pictures may make good stained-glass windows but they rarely have any saving power! The somewhat idealised portrayal of family relationships in Ecclesiasticus (3:2-7) is balanced by the Exodus story (12:21-27) of salvation for the family — but only through sacrifice.

So, of what did the holiness of the 'Holy Family' consist? The Collect is right, of course, there was an amazing amount of love and obedience exercised within it. It was as true then as it is now that holiness does not flourish on neglected family responsibilities — a factor remembered by our Lord not only in boyhood but also *in extremis* when he committed the care of his mother to his loving disciple, John. But surely it consisted primarily in God's choice of that family, his presence within it, and his purpose for it. God had chosen Abraham in order that a nation would be blessed. He chose Mary to be the mother, and together with Joseph, to be the guardians of the one who, in the words of our second Collect, was to be the light of the nations.

God is the source of all holiness. He is also the one from whom every family (or his whole family) in heaven and earth derives its name. That may mean, quite simply, that he is the father of the Church both living and departed, and we, as Ephesians reminds us, who carry his name are called to be his sons and daughters and to bear the family likeness.

If that is the full content of its meaning, then the vision of Revelation will be narrower than would first appear (Revelation 21:22-22:5). In an increasingly pluralist society, can we with integrity so easily dismiss God from his relation to, and his intimate concern for, the vast majority of the world's population? Is there nothing positive to say to the devout Muslim family, or indeed to the self-confessed secular family whose love for each other and whose service to the community so often puts many Christian families in the shade? Furthermore, what are we to say to those far from idyllic, but all too frequent situations where families are broken, embittered or estranged? God does not abandon his creation. If he is present in those situations, then is there not always the possibility that holiness may flourish?

Perhaps it is at this point that the 'Holy Family' can provide not an idyllic picture but a practical help. Within all family life there is the ideal and there is the reality, and most of us struggle somewhere between the two. The Epiphany element in another of today's gospels (Matthew 2:1-12, 19-23) reminds us of the light which burned in the midst of the 'Holy Family' and which shone for all the world. The story tells of wise men who followed a star, and having seen that light, 'departed to their own country by another way'. Though that is simply a statement of fact, it describes the experience of disciples and pilgrims of every age. It is in Christ's light that we see light, and it is in following that light that we grow in holiness and wholeness — both as individuals and as families.

Epiphany

The Adoration of the Kings

Donald Reeves

A PART from churches, which are often locked, art galleries are the only places where Christianity is publicly celebrated. In the National Gallery there is a sumptuous painting by the Dutch painter Gossaert, *The Adoration of the Kings*, which celebrates today's festival of the Epiphany.

This picture is a striking reminder of how familiar biblical stories have always been clothed for their own day. (In the National Gallery, there are other quite different interpretations of the Epiphany — one by Bruegel and another by Botticelli). Gossaert has three Kings: Caspar kneels in front of Mary, with his gift of gold. Melchior with his companions presents myrrh. Balthazar, the black King, offers frankincense. Parts of the Christmas story are mixed up in all this: Joseph looks on, there is an ass, and an ox, and a glimpse of some shepherds and sheep. In the sky the angels sing the *Gloria*; and in the very centre of the picture there is the star.

But in Matthew's story, the bearers of the gifts have no names. They are not kings. They are astrologers — the wisest of the wise, and Matthew does not say how many astrologers there were.

Matthew is not an original writer. He embellishes motifs from the Old Testament: 'The Kings of Tarshish and of the Isles shall give presents: the Kings of Arabia and Sala shall bring gifts.' There is also a direct allusion to an Old Testament story: Moses is leading the people to the promised land. He meets a wicked king, Balak of Moab, who wants to destroy him. Balak summons from the East a famous foreign magician, Balaam, to help him. They come, but instead of cursing Moses, Balaam says, 'There shall come a man out of Israel's seed, and he shall rule many nations ... I see him, but not now. I behold him, but not close; a star shall rise from Jacob and a man shall come forth from Israel.' (Numbers 24:7,17) David is the star that Balaam had foreseen

— the one who would be the true King, and later these verses were taken to be a reference to the Messiah, the anointed one from David's ancestors.

But only the astrologers understand. Herod is troubled and 'all Jerusalem with him' — a hint of the passion to come.

The appeal of this story lies, as so many pictures of the Epiphany show, in the powerful, the rich and the wise together with the poor, the shepherds and all creation — the sheep, the oxen and cows and the asses worshipping and adoring the Christ Child. It is this which evokes a capacity to search for the truth and to worship God whoever we are, and wherever we are from.

The story does not make dogmatic statements. It is not a lecture in doctrine or theology. It does not bully or cajole its readers into saying that the only way to God is through Jesus Christ. The story is that of testimony, and confession; it is a paean of love, a response to what was revealed of God in Christ, assimilated and written down after the Ressurrection.

First Sunday
after the Epiphany

∽

Revelation:
The Baptism of Jesus

Richard Holloway

SCHOLARS dispute with each other about the various incidents of our Lord's life. Some take a highly sceptical attitude to the historical status of much that is recorded, while others accord to the New Testament a high degree of historical validity. They all use different canons of verification, different ways of assessing the likely status of particular stories. One of these tests might be called the 'embarrassment test'. If an incident in our Lord's life or one of his sayings is the kind of thing that would have caused difficulty for the early Church, the thinking goes, we can be fairly certain that it is authentic, because the editorial tendency would have been in the opposite direction in selecting stories. By the test of embarrassment or difficulty, then, the account of our Lord's baptism is authentic, because it must have been a bit of an embarrassment to the early Church. It was reported and therefore recorded, but it must have been puzzling to the first Christians, because they believed strongly in the sinlessness of Jesus, yet here he is submitting to a baptism by John the great prophet of repentance. It may be, indeed, that John's embarrassment in the gospel accounts is a reflection of this difficulty: 'I need to be baptized by you, and do you come to me?', Matthew describes John as saying (Matthew 3:14).

There are at least two meanings to be found in the story. In Matthew's account, Jesus tells John that 'it is fitting for us to fulfil all righteousness' (Matthew 3:15). Part of that righteousness is repentance, amendment of life, a radical turning away from the self and a turning outward to God and his children. That was John's great message. Like the great prophets of old, he thundered against a purely formal or ritualistic religion in which discipleship was reduced to certain cultic activities or certain mental attitudes. For John, the great test of pure religion was righteousness and justice. God, he warned his hearers, made moral demands upon them and they would be judged by their obedience to these demands. There is, therefore, a strongly ethical strain in prophetic religion and Jesus identified with it at his baptism. We could say that his baptism was an act of solidarity with the great call of the prophets for moral and social righteousness. By his baptism, therefore, Jesus affirmed the need for right conduct, moral behaviour and the duty to act justly towards others.

But if that is all we are given, then we are left with a religion of law that can reduce us to impotence and despair. Part of our human tragedy is that, knowing the right thing to do, we often find no power within ourselves to do it. The real dilemma for human beings is not *knowing* the right, but *doing* the right. Even more important for us is what we do with ourselves when we *know* we are in the wrong, have no righteousness, and can only lift our eyes to God and ask him to be merciful to us sinners. And this is where Jesus went beyond John, from the importance of law to the necessity of grace. If John was the prophet of the wilderness, Jesus was the beloved son of the God of mercy, anointed with that very spirit that fills up our lack with the grace of God.

In his baptism, therefore, Jesus not only fulfilled all righteousness and affirmed the necessity of the ethical; he was also anointed by God for the fulfilment of his mission to redeem those who had lost all power to save themselves.

Second Sunday
after the Epiphany

The First Disciples

Donald Reeves

THE unconditional character of discipleship, which is found in one of today's gospel readings (Mark 1:14-20) could not have been expressed more directly; it involves nothing less than an absolute break with family and occupation. James and John, both fishermen, are 'called'. They leave their father in the boat where they had been mending nets and, as Mark puts it tersely, 'went off to follow him'. In an ancient, oriental culture, it was more natural for a rabbi or prophet to invite a student to study with him, even to live in the master's home.

However, the strangeness of this compressed narrative becomes clearer in the context of some of the other readings for today. The first is Jeremiah's call (Jeremiah 1:4-10). Jeremiah was also a reluctant prophet. He feels inadequate: 'I do not know how to speak; I am only a child.' To which the Lord, somewhat brusquely, replies, 'Do not call yourself a child; for you shall go to whatever people I send you and say whatever I tell you to say.'

The second is Paul's account of his conversion (Acts 26 1:9-20). Paul was literally turned round — from the active persecution of the followers of Jesus Christ to becoming the one who was largely responsible for the rapid spread of Christianity in the Mediterranean.

The disciples did not ask to be disciples. Jeremiah was not cut out to be a prophet, and Paul was busy punishing Christians. In other words, the initiative for these radical changes comes from God.

There are many who would call themselves seekers — men and women searching for God, as if God was a lost golf ball. They hope they will stumble against God, and thus find God. But that is to denigrate the Jewish/Christian tradition, for it is more accurate to say that we are found by God. It is God who ambushes us, takes us by surprise in many different ways. 'It is a dreadful thing to fall into the hands of the living God' (Hebrews 10:31). God so often turns the tables on us. As if we were the hunters, we suddenly find ourselves the hunted ones. Discipleship begins as a response to this prompting from God; it is a response freely given, but the initiative comes beyond or deep within ourselves.

It is easy to forget the unconditional nature of Christianity. Conversion is not just a matter of welcoming Christ as Lord and Saviour into our hearts: it is a personal, but never private, experience — for the Christian aspires to bring everything under the Lordship of Christ. If Christ is Lord, then politics, economics, work, relationships, our attitude to animals and creation, all have to be subject to the claims of the Kingdom of God, central to the teaching of Jesus Christ. And while Jesus continually speaks of the Kingdom in his parables and miracles, and especially in the way he invited the poor and everyone on the margins of society to discover their dignity, there is no blueprint for the Kingdom. That has to be worked out again and again and that involves an unconditional commitment — but we are assured, as Jeremiah puts it, 'I am with you and will keep you safe'.

Third Sunday
after the Epiphany

Revelation:
Signs of Glory

Michael Sadgrove

IT is the Fourth Gospel that speaks of 'signs' (*not* miracles) that
Jesus performs in order that the glory of God may be revealed.
Fittingly, then, both gospel readings for Years 1 and 2 in the
Eucharist are taken from St. John: the story of the wedding at
Cana in Galilee, and the feeding of the crowd. In addition, the
New Testament reading in Year 1 is from the First Letter of John,
so that the theology of the Fourth Evangelist may truly be said
to permeate the readings for today.

The Year 1 readings offer us a fascinating account of the word
'glory'. The Old Testament reading (Exodus 33:12-end), in
particular, is vital for our understanding of what St. John means
when he uses this great biblical word. It records a dialogue
between God and Moses ('face to face, as someone speaks to a
friend', says the passage earlier on) in which Moses makes the
universal religious demand: 'show me your glory, I beg you.' In
this text, the 'glory' of God (the root meaning of the Hebrew word
is 'weight') is associated with two things specifically: his
compassion, and his name *Yahweh*. But, says God, Moses cannot
set eyes on the face of God; for that would be (in T.S. Eliot's
words) 'too much reality'; he can only glimpse the glory of God
as he passes by.

Against that background, St. John's claim that in the
Incarnation, 'we have beheld his glory . . . full of grace and truth'
(John 1:14) is seen as the powerful and radical claim that it is.
For that which human eyes could not gaze upon has now been
fully and finally disclosed to the world in Jesus. That is what gives
both the New Testament reading and the Gospel for today their
point. In one of the readings (1 John 1:1-7), the author is careful
to point out that the Incarnation makes God present as visible,
tangible and accessible. The Gospel (John 2:1-11) establishes the
same truth by telling the story of the first 'sign' Jesus performed

41

as he began his ministry. The traditional Epiphany story of the marriage of Cana contains many characteristic Johannine themes: water, wine, Christ's 'hour'; but supreme is the revelation of his glory, the disclosure to his disciples of his true nature and mission. And just as in so many places in the Fourth Gospel (John 1:12; 3:16-18; 20:31), so here, disclosure is to lead to *faith* in him whom God has sent to be the Saviour of the world.

The Year 2 readings form a less coherent group. The secondary theme is that of God providing for his people: in the wilderness (Deuteronomy 8:1-6), in life and ministry (Philippians 4:10-20) and, ultimately, in Christ himself (John 6:1-14). In this latter story from the Fourth Gospel, the feeding of the five thousand, the word 'sign' is again used; and the discourse that follows today's reading again establishes the need for faith in Christ the Living Bread from God (John 6:35-40). No doubt this passage would have been heard in the early Church as a vivid picture of the Eucharist. But so far as today's theme is concerned, it underlines the message of the wedding at Cana (perhaps also not without its eucharistic overtones?) — that the glory of God is revealed in ways that are — paradoxically — material, ordinary, workaday. That is the truth of the Incarnation. St. John brings his Gospel to its climax as he presents us with the ultimate paradox of all: that it is in the cross that the glory of God shines out in all its splendour. It is at the cross that the long search behind Moses' cry 'show me your glory' finds its goal. For there we contemplate the glory of love poured out for the world, the glory of a crucified God who reigns as King.

Fourth Sunday after Epiphany

〜

The New Temple

Paul Oestreicher

THROUGHOUT history the great master-builders have gone to the limits of human artistry and creativity in their attempts to express the inexpressible: the glory of God. We can only imagine what Solomon's Temple was like. We can go to York and experience the breath-taking beauty of its Minster. We can go to Russia and await the day — which will surely come — when the dazzlingly beautiful Kremlin Cathedrals will once again be filled with the majesty of the Divine Liturgy and the mystery of clouds of incense. How we long to place our God on the most glorious of thrones. In a sense, the truth of our faith seems to depend on the splendour of our Cathedrals, the glory of our music, the solemnity of our ritual. I cannot forget it, worshipping day by day in Coventry Cathedral, a moving monument in stone to the Christ of the 20th century. But then I hear Jeremiah saying to the people of Israel: 'You keep saying: this place is the temple of the Lord, the temple of the Lord, the temple of the Lord! This catchword of yours is a lie ... mend your ways ... deal fairly with one another, do not oppress the alien ... you gain nothing by putting your trust in this lie. You steal, you murder, you commit adultery ... and you think you are safe? Do you think this house that bears my name is a robbers cave?' (Jeremiah 7:1-11) And, echoing these words, Jesus drove the profiteers out of the Temple in a piece of bold and — for himself — very dangerous direct action.

How easy it is, indeed how easy religion makes it, to mistake the trapping for the real thing. The Spirit of the living God cannot be locked in cages of gold or even in autere protestant chapels or the simplest of Quaker meeting houses. 'Do you not know that you are God's temple and that God's Spirit dwells in you?', St. Paul asks the Christians in Corinth. (1 Corinthians 3:10-17)

We are outraged by the desecration of a church. Are we half

43

as outraged when some helpless refugee is humiliated by our immigration officials simply doing their job?

How we treat strangers says far more about our relation to God than how much money we put into the upkeep of our places of worship. Victor Hugo recognised that 'the quality of a nations's life is determined not by the state of its churches but by the state of its prisons'. If every human being, and therefore every prisoner, is in some profound sense God's dwelling place, if George Fox was right in insisting on the honour due to 'that of God in every person' then might the time not long be overdue when Christians say: Not another penny for church renovation until we have paid for an end to the degrading conditions in our prisons?

It is — or should be — crystal clear that Jesus wants to be honoured not in monuments of stone but in the least of our sisters and brothers. In some Christian traditions it is an ancient custom to genuflect or bow to Christ, present in the sacramental bread and wine, his body and blood. How strange then that these same Christians fail to genuflect and bow even to each other in whom this divine body and blood lives. In fact, of course, we should treat all people as though they were God because in some profound, mystical sense that is what they are . . . or, if not God, then made in his image. And that is the one true ground for Christian self-respect, that God dwells in each of us, that we are living temples of the Holy Spirit. Ultimately, in the heavenly Jerusalem, that will be self-evident. There will be no Temple of stone to confuse the issue.

Fifth Sunday
after Epiphany

Revelation:
The Wisdom of God

Neville Clark

TO be hailed as the embodiment of wisdom would give most of us pleasure. Being clever may sound faintly disreputable, even vaguely suspect. Wisdom, however, is very definitely an okay word.

So, lured by the attractive prospect and mindful of the encouragement that the Jesus of Matthew's Gospel seems to offer (Matthew 12:38-42), we join the Queen of Sheba's caravan en route to Solomon's court and, courtesy of the Book of Proverbs, sample a course in wisdom (Proverbs 2:1-9). Everything is clearcut. Once we opt for insight and understanding, we emerge with the key to righteousness and justice, with God and his favour thrown in for good measure. Certainly this is value for money. Indeed, it prepares us to sit at the feet of the gospel of the Kingdom of God that Jesus brings. He is the Wisdom of God. At his coming and at the message he voices, something greater than Solomon confronts us.

To be sure, into this harmonious situation Paul the apostle seems to intrude like a jangling discord (1 Corinthians 3:18-end). From him the 'wise' do seem to get a bad press. Folly and foolishness seems to be his preferred option. Momentarily nonplussed, we reassure ourselves with the reflection that he was after all breaking a lance with 'the wisdom of this world'. That, fortunately, is not the kind of wisdom we wish to deal in. Worldly wisdom is the sort of commodity in which the irreligious traffic. Too clever by half! And God left out of account!

All loose ends now seem tied up. Yet before we tiptoe away, going out exactly where we came in, suppose we play safe and once more recheck the Gospel bearings. On the one side, evil scribes and Pharisees, flushed with the wisdom of this world, seeking some evidential sign of the truth of Jesus. On the other side, repentant Nineveh and questing Sheba (plus you and I) attentive to the wisdom from on high. What could be fairer than that — and more predictable. A classic picture of faith versus unbelief.

The trouble is that everything depends on where you locate *yourself.* Look over the shoulder of those scribes and Pharisees for a moment — religious men, all. They want a 'sign'. That is our kind of language. Some definite guidance, some clearcut answer to prayer — to give unmistakable indication that God is on the field. And are they not 'wise' to seek credentials? When a dozen conflicting faiths contend, you might be sadly led astray if you back the first horse that comes along. Some means of discrimination seems in order.

Is that, after all, why Jesus specialises in parables? A parable is a story of life as we know it. It lures us along familiar ground, the commonsense world of our experience where native wisdom rules. Until, suddenly, the Kingdom of God and its summons intrudes like a lightning flash, turning things upside down, making the ground tremble, upsetting our neat expectations, demanding unpredictable response. There is no escape from the choice. The problem is always in determining which is the road of foolishness and which the path of a wisdom that looks strangely like folly.

Sixth Sunday after the Epiphany

Revelation: Parables

Gordon Mursell

FROM groups of devout Jews, maintaining their faith under persecution by retelling the Exodus story, to the millions who tune in every week to 'The Archers' or 'Dallas', people have never lost their appetite for stories. Like other great religious teachers, Jesus constantly used them to convey profound truth; and stories like the Prodigal Son and the Good Samaritan have never lost their capacity to communicate and challenge.

There are various reasons for this. First, stories collide with, and address, our own experience, however distant their subject matter might appear to be. The word 'parable' comes from a Greek word meaning 'to set side by side'. The heart of the Eucharist is precisely this collision between the story of the Last Supper — the story of Jesus — and our own stories. Sometimes that collision can be painful. The passage from 2 Samuel 12:1-10 graphically illustrates our propensity to denounce in others the sins we fail to discern within ourselves; and Nathan's response to David's self-righteous anger exemplifies the way God uses stories to cut through our easy complacency and address our own experience.

Secondly, stories speak to our imagination. There are really two ways in which we can use words to communicate truth to others. One is through the language of *concept*; the other is through the language of *image*. Though he could use image language with great effect when he wanted to, St. Paul seems to have preferred the language of concept; and in the passage from Romans 1:18-25, he rightly warns the Christians in Rome of the dangers of 'exchanging the splendour of immortal God' for images of created things. Despite their limitations, however, images have a capacity to evoke and attract and challenge that concepts never have. The teaching of Jesus is laced with the salty, earthy imagery of life in rural Galilee. Much contemporary Christian worship has

47

sacrificed the rich and many-sided allusiveness of image language for the chilly precision of concepts. The earthy immediacy of the image in Cranmer's Confession ('We have erred and strayed from thy ways like lost sheep'), for example, is lost in the exact, but dull, modern equivalent ('We have sinned ... through negligence, through weakness, through our own deliberate fault'). We urgently need to find ways of restoring the imaginative dimension to Christian worship; and the telling or sharing of stories is one way to do it.

Which brings us to the most important point of all. The real reason we find stories irresistible is because all of us have one. Not everyone has a doctorate in divinity or a knowledge of New Testament Greek. But everyone has a story; and all that is needed, in hearing the parables of Jesus or the stories in the Bible, is a willingness to let them touch your own. When Jesus wanted to explain to people the nature of the kingdom of heaven, he didn't deliver a lecture on eschatology. He told a story. By learning to discern and acknowledge both the wheat and the weeds within our own lives, we allow that story to collide with ours; and, when that happens, our own experience and stories become places of encounter with the risen Christ, and living parables for the world today.

Ninth Sunday before Easter

Christ the Teacher

Peter Firth

A teacher is someone who helps you to understand and/or do something for yourself. He releases thoughts and actions of which you did not know you were capable.

But often, teaching comes to us in the form of rules imposed on us. This may make us obedient — through fear of the consequences if we break the rules — but it is bad teaching. The Ten Commandments were given so that people should have a happier way of life together. If you *reverse* the Ten Commandments and say: 'Thou *shalt* kill, steal, commit adultery, betray your neighbour and covet his or her possessions', you will see how chaotic life would become, and how full of fear, jealousy, anger and uncertainty.

The Beatitudes and Parables of Jesus are a way of saying: 'This is the way of truth and happiness. If you explore life in these ways, you will give your life a firm and fearless centre. If you choose the opposite, you will enter a maze of jealousy and suspicion which will gradually kill your capacity *for* love and your capacity *to* love. But the choice is yours.

Following the teaching of Jesus is not easy. Others will think your honesty and truthfulness are naïve. They will see your purity of heart as an attack on their own slyness and lust for pleasure. You will be seen as 'unrealistic and idealistic', as Jesus was by the 'practical' religious men of his day. You will have to guard against seeming to think yourself better than others, when you know that you are not. And you will often feel powerless in a world which judges by appearances, and only seems to respect power and money. You will, like St. Paul, often be judged as a fool — for Christ's sake.

But you will learn to be afraid of nothing and no-one. The teaching of Jesus — all his parables and sayings, all his actions and relationships — have one end and aim: to enable you to live without fear and without shame, in a world which accepts these cancers of the heart as the price to be paid for looking after Number One.

Nearly sixteen hundred years ago, St. Augustine asked the question: 'Is a thing good because God says so, or do we come to recognise the Presence of God by the intrinsic goodness (or rightness) of a thing?' He plumped for the latter, because he believed that we have to *choose* the things we respect and value, the things that make for love, the things of the Kingdom.

And that is what a good teacher always does. He says: 'These thoughts, these actions, make for happiness and life. The opposite leads to darkness and death of the spirit. Choose life.' In other words, he makes goodness attractive and the things of God desirable, rather than the result of obedience to a despot or a life of boring duty. He plants good seed amongst the weeds of life and leaves us the freedom — and the power — to make them grow. He enables us to *make* the love he offers.

Eighth Sunday before Easter

Christ the Healer

Peter Firth

THE ministry of Jesus had one aim above all others — Healing. He enabled people to relate freely and lovingly with God — and with each other. He showed the connection between the touch of love and wholeness of mind and body. And although he didn't automatically link suffering with sin (John 9:2-3), he showed that certain sins do affect the body and their forgiveness can bring healing of body as well as of soul. (Mark 2:1-12).

Healing usually begins when serious illness is recognised. If you won't admit that you *are* ill, that you *have* got a temperature, a broken leg, things are likely to get worse — even to death. And if you can't see that all of us are fallible, fragile creatures — even the apparently strongest — the healing of relationships, 'the minds fractured by life', the guilt-ridden, the fearful, as well as the physically ill becomes difficult and sometime impossible.

You only have to look at the face of people coming through a super-market checkout, or standing at a bus stop, to see how much we need healing. Life has written many harsh lines on our faces — the faces of the proud as well as those of the down-trodden.

And God wants to renew the beauty he wrote on our faces when we were children. He knows that life is hard and that we make a mess of things over and over again. To some he says 'I have taken away the judgements against you' (Zephaniah 3:15); to others he says 'the prayer of faith will save the sick man ... if he has committed sins, he will be forgiven' (James 5:15). To a paralysed man brought into his presence he says 'your sins are forgiven ... take up your bed and walk' (Mark 2:10). To a stranger in the Holy Land he says 'my healing is for all — not just for special people' (2 Kings 5). And through St. Paul, God shows that it is when we are weak and feel inadequate that he identifies with us most — as he did on the Cross. That horror which is Calvary is his way of saying: 'I know what it is like to be in physical pain and an outcast — it is out of that condition that new life comes. So, hang on; offer me your weakness; I have known it all. And I have come to bring you life, even when you are helpless. Trust me. Your faith is the doorway to wholeness.'

Healing requires humility. The humility to admit sickness and our inability to deal with it alone. The humility to put yourself in someone else's hands in order to achieve the health and wholeness we desire and need. And whether this means going to a doctor or admitting failure or sin, the process is the same. Healing is the restoring of that which has broken down. And whether this is to do with the cells of the body or the fragile elements of a relationship — or the relations between management and workers, or national governments — healing and health can only begin when breakdown is admitted and failure is forgiven.

Jesus is God's good news that healing on all these levels *is* possible. He is God's witness to the healing power and endurance of love, and its public face — justice. Love will always be the greatest healing agent of all.

Seventh Sunday
before Easter

*Christ the Friend
of Sinners*

Peter Firth

'GOD will forgive it', wrote a French philosopher, 'it is his job.' but however naïve and facile that may sound, it is a continuing experience for a Christian.

The things of creation have no option as to how they behave. Flowers must bloom, rain must fall, earthquakes must happen, and mosquitoes must bite. The laws of nature are as they are, and no part of nature has the power or the free will to disobey them. Nature's harmony is natural — except where *people* are concerned.

Our harmony has to be thought out and worked for. We have two dangerous capacities which nature does not have. We can *distinguish* between right and wrong, and we have the ability — and the power — to *choose* what to do. Harmony between people, and between us and God, does not just happen. We *make* it happen, by choosing to treat other people as we would like to be treated; and by living the kind of life we believe to be in harmony with the God who is love. We *make* the love which binds us together in harmony.

Sin is a denial of that harmony, of 'how things should be'. Sin is 'missing the target', 'getting it wrong'. It is usually the result of a limited, selfish and self-centred view of what is right. And even when our sins are private and seem to harm no-one, we bring to all our decisions and relationship the mind and character of 'a sinner'.

The glory of biblical faith is that although we weave sinful knots which justice and reason can rarely undo without a punishment, there is a way of dissolving the knots. It is the way of *penitence*. Of saying: 'yes, I was wrong to do/say/think that. I am sorry. Forgive me.' It sounds easy, but it is based on a recognition of reality — we *have* sinned; we *do* see that; we *are* sorry; we ask to be forgiven — both by God and our neighbour.

This is the experience of countless people in the Bible. God says 'I will receive you back', wrote Hosea, 'if you will be honest about your sins.' 'If your slave Onesiphorus returns to you', wrote St. Paul to Philemon, 'you *will* receive him back without punishment because his return is his apology, and God has received you back.' 'I am eating with sinners', said Jesus to Simon the Pharisee, 'because they *know* they are at fault; the so-called virtuous don't!'

And whereas the Old Testament in cruder times saw punishments as fitting crimes, and called for the stoning of those who abused the Sabbath (Numbers 15:32-36), Jesus separated the sin from the penitent sinner, withheld condemnation and simply said 'don't do it again'.

The forgiveness which follows 'I'm sorry' is the golden cord of love which God substitutes for the knot. God says: 'I know you are fallible creatures, who abuse your precious freedom and go for wrong targets, but my love for you is so firm that I allow it to be nailed to a cross, rather than cut you off. And as my love is life itself, I beg you — through the humility of a crucifixion — to acknowledge what you have done, and start again. I will enable you to start again — through forgiveness.' That is what *reconciliation* means.

The Pharisee in the Temple (Luke 18:9-14), who thought that his prayers and alms-giving made him right with God, had missed the point. It was the publican, who could only muster 'God be merciful to me a sinner', who went home without knots, to start life again . . . and again . . . and again . . .

Ash Wednesday

'Lord, Have Mercy'

Rodney Matthews

WE are not left guessing who is arrested by the parable in Luke 18:9-14. Luke tells us that it was 'aimed at those who were sure of their own goodness and looked down on everyone else'. Ash Wednesday is the day for self-abasement, the donning of sackcloth and ashes, the penitent's paradise. But therein lies the danger! The dividing line between righteousness and self-righteousness is thin, even invisible. So Jesus provides one of his brilliant caricatures to explode hypocrisy.

Who needs this as the saintly sinners slip silently into Church to begin Lent? Is this a parable about 'them' or 'us'? It is clear who is in the right (the wrongdoer!), but how close to the wind do we sail as the righteous who may just be wrong? There is our dilemma.

It cannot be wrong to respond to the call to love the Lord our God with all our heart and soul and strength and mind. We are inclined to view Pharisees as hypocrites, but at their best they were not motivated by anything less than that which draws us away from the crowds and into the heady atmosphere of the presence of God. And, once there, do we not feel just a tinge of one-upmanship, that out there is the world of sin and in here is the holy of holies, and we have 'chosen that good part', which shall not be taken away from us? We even like to be noticed in our choice and call it witness. We will show the world the way and you cannot do that without being seen. And just in case God may be nodding off, we give him a nudge to remind him that we are the faithful few still sighing. It is good to be here! Are we wrong to think we're right?

We must by now be used to the topsy turvey world of the Kingdom, the back-to-front, inside-out state where the mirrored image invariably turns the negative into the positive. That is not to say that we may not be surprised by the surprising — for that would be the contradiction to end all contradictions. The gospel turns us round and round until our heads spin with giddiness and we sink to our knees before we fall down altogether. Let it happen, for when we are helpless to stand we may be in the best position to pray.

Now consider the cutting edge of the gospel of James (4:1-10). If the world is your friend, God is your enemy, he says. God is opposed to the proud but offers help to the humble. Clean your hands. Clear your thinking. Weep in misery. But careful! It is not the motions of the hypocrite that appeal to God. See Isaiah 58:1-8, where pretence is exposed and the 'righteous' are sent back into the world to do right in the sight of God who has appeared not to notice their empty gesture of fasting in a hungry world.

We are brought back at last to the parable and the simple conclusion (isn't that another of the gospel's surprises, that it is always so straightforward?), that upon a genuine confession of sin in a sinful world, the cry for mercy, comes the peace of acquittal. He who genuinely falls on his knees before God is raised to his feet again and set free from himself.

First Sunday
of Lent

The King and the Kingdom: Temptation

Neville Clark

TEMPTATION is an ugly word. It conjures up a picture of devilish and satanic jiggery-pokery, with men and women doing battle against almost impossible odds. Evil takes centre-stage. The price of moral survival becomes constant vigilance. We enter the inheritance of countless christian centuries where serpents and apples and women and nudity are confusedly mixed in a Genesis production, and the whole is glossed by the profound if unsuspected influence of Milton's *Paradise Lost* (Genesis 2:7-9). We take comfort from the assurance of the Letter to the Hebrews that Jesus himself knew the battle and therefore can stand helpfully with us (Hebrews 2:14-end). Lent, we conclude, may be a suitable occasion for once more girding our armour on.

Maybe we need to revise our strategy and our perspective. Maybe we need to puncture the inflated pretensions of evil. Maybe we need to look away and concentrate on falling in love with goodness by exposing ourselves to its magnetic attraction. However that be, it may be important to see Jesus as a guide to the problem and not simply as a resource for its triumphant solution. If we begin with the Gospel, what shall we find?

Life is a matter of normal and necessary choices. So here, in the wake of a baptism and a commission it has imposed, rise inevitable suggestions about what to do and how to manage. The test itself is wholly familiar. It relates to choices that have to be made and the inevitable uncertainty that always attends significant choice (Matthew 4:1-11).

What is the key to human fulfilment? A contented stomach? You had better start with that, lest there be nowhere else beyond to go. The multitudes must be fed. But you cannot finish with that. There is a deeper necessity still; and its name is God. 'Not by bread alone'!

What is the road to human fulfilment? If God and his Kingdom is the end, what is the means? Impressive display? Good theatre? The kind of magic people always fall for? But what if the end is already embedded in the means, as the oak in the acorn and the flower in the bulb? Again Jesus reached into a nation's tangled past, and hazarded a choice. You had to manage God's way to come out anywhere in God's neighbourhood.

So what are the odds on human fulfilment? Since whoever rules in the human cities it is not God, the goal is impossible of attainment. Face the facts. Evil is centre-stage. Unless you acknowledge that, you live in a dream world, and the end is defeat and disillusionment. And Jesus chose defeat — with God; and wagered that somehow it might conceal an impossible victory.

To make the significant choices of our daily living by opting for the Kingdom via the ways of the Kingdom is to face a struggle whose beating heart is uncertainty; the goal unclear; the road unsignposted; and long odds on victorious fulfilment. We call the struggle, temptation. We call the choice, faith. We call the victory, the Cross.

Second Sunday in Lent

॰॰॰

The King and the Kingdom: Conflict

Neville Clark

THE Lenten march towards Easter is the story of what happens when God comes in power. That sovereign rule that we call the Kingdom of God is on the field. However much we may find scripture obscure, here we are back on familiar ground. We know where we are when there is talk of kingdoms. Flags to be planted; bugles to be blown; trumpets to be sounded; enemies to be engaged; Elgar's *Pomp and Circumstance* as background music. It's just a question of making sure you are on the right and winning side.

Would that it were that simple! The trouble is that already two yellow lights are flashing, warning us to proceed with caution. In the first instance, it is an odd kind of power that God seems to favour. The bearer and embodiment of the Kingdom is this Nazareth carpenter whose legions seem conspicuous by their absence. His firepower seems oddly ineffective, by whatever slide-rule you measure it. He comes to engage Jerusalem, so the Gospel writer would have us believe, with tears in his eyes! That of course strikes a chord. The weapon of love. You can't get more Christian than that. Only, just when we feel that after all we have got it taped, the tears become a prelude to driving money changers from the Temple. So that even the power of love has somehow to be redefined, ceasing to be some warm emotion that has forgotten how to be severe, even with itself.

By the time we have interpreted that yellow light, our triumphant victory train has slowed to a crawl. Now that other yellow light is flashing. Are we, after all, in the right carriage? Are we even in the right train? On the face of it, the scriptural travel agents seemed to have given us clear instructions. In the clash of kingdoms, the conflict between God and his world, we knew just where we were and who we were. We were faithful Noah, piling into the Ark in unqualified obedience, ready to float

59

beyond judgement. We were the 'little children' assured by letter-writer John that we were 'of God', backing the 'spirit of truth' against the 'spirit of error'. Certainly we were among those weeping with Jesus over the unrepentant Jerusalem city. Unthinkable that we insiders could be outsiders, that we could be part of heedless Jerusalem, resistant to the spirit of truth, with the flood waters brushing our ankles — when God comes in strange and curious power. Unthinkable?

Maybe everything depends on where you join the train and how you identify your place in this topsy-turvy scenario. Maybe this clearcut controversy and conflict between God and his world calls for some searing self-questioning, if you are to locate where in reality you belong. Maybe discriminating between arks and escape-hatches, discerning where truth actually lies, and identifying where Jesus the Christ currently stands on the Long March of the Kingdom, demand a sensitive openness to scripture's challenges and a constant willingness to be surprised.

Third Sunday of Lent

The King and the Kingdom: Suffering

Gordon Mursell

WHY do innocent people suffer? Why is life so manifestly unfair? No religious tradition has ever provided a completely satisfying answer to these questions, and doubtless none ever could. But the Judaeo-Christian tradition has shown an unflinching readiness to live with the questions, and refuse to escape their challenge. The sheer grinding unfairness of life, and its seemingly random or arbitrary character, are mirrored in the Bible from start to finish: why did God choose Abraham, and not the Canaanites (Genesis 12:1-9)? Why did he allow Isaac to be submitted to such a grim ordeal in the land of Moriah (Gensis 22:1-13)? Why did the Son of Man have to suffer so grievously (Luke 9:18-27)? The questions are not directly answered. What is offered instead is the presence of the living God in the heart of the suffering, taking upon himself the cruel unfairness that afflicts so many of his people — not so that they no longer have to suffer, but precisely so as to give them courage to endure.

Yet endurance is not all the Jewish and Christian traditions have to say about suffering. Two other resources are offered for all victims of suffering, whatever its cause: protest, and praise.

The urge to protest is one of the deepest instincts in creatures, human and animal alike; and one of the first things a child learns to do is to protest when it is forcibly separated from its mother. In the Bible that cry of protest becomes prayer. In the Psalms, the Book of Job, in Gethsemane, and in the last moments of Jesus' earthly life, intense suffering finds expression not just in a prayer of endurance but in a prayer of protest. Why is this happening, Lord? God, why have you forsaken me? Why can't you get me out of here? What have I done to deserve this? And, most of all, why me? If our prayer and worship are to address people's experience as it really is, there must be room within them for this honest expression of doubt and protest. Without it, we run the risk of pasteurising human experience, not transforming it.

The other response to suffering reflected throughout the Bible is praise. Down the centuries, millions of Jews and Christians alike have responded to terrible suffering by praising or blessing the name of the Lord. They were not thanking God for sending the suffering. What they were doing was saying, in effect, that not even the most terrible torment can cut you off from the love of God; and that, in the end, that love will triumph. From the psalmist to the gulag, from Gethsemane to Auschwitz and Soweto, Jews and Christians have baffled their adversaries by praising God even in the midst of their suffering. This is not easy escapism. It's the conviction that, whatever happens to them, the power of evil will not ultimately prevail. That is the 'hidden secret' of which St Paul speaks in the letter to the Colossians: 'Christ in you, the hope of a glory to come.' (Colossians 1:24-end)

Fourth Sunday of Lent

The King and the Kingdom: Transfiguration

Robert Williamson

MAJESTY and suffering would appear to be mutually exclusive. They certainly do not combine in ways which the secular world can easily understand. Normally it is the powerless who suffer, and as they are also usually the voiceless and the choiceless, they tend to be banished to the margins of society. Death and glory are an even more unlikely pair to be linked, unless we are wedded to an outmoded nationalism. Death is normally seen as the ultimate triumph of evil, rather than the final accolade of the good life.

Such wordly wisdom is far removed from authentic Christian faith and tradition. In the person and work of our Lord, the mutually exclusive became a necessary and redemptive combination. As the Servant King, his majesty was not only revealed before the cross but, in a quite remarkable way, in and through the cross. The cross became the event which portrayed above all else the extent of his commitment to serve.

Majesty was a concept with which Old Testament believers were familiar. Not for them the 'mateyness' of some present day believers, who seem to have no compunction in telling God what to do, and who, to all intents and purposes, seem to clothe him in jumpers and jeans and treat him as one of the boys! No, in the Old Testament, and indeed in the New, there is an awesomeness — and it comes through loud and clear in today's readings. It is an element which needs to be re-discovered and retained rather than lost in modern spirituality. As both Moses and Paul discovered, the closer we get to God the greater is our awareness of his majesty and glory and of our need to 'put off our shoes' in reverential response.

Showing clearly through all our readings today is the amazing truth that something of the glory, or outworked character, of God can be transferred to us and that we, increasingly, can be transformed by it. Nowhere is this more specifically and sublimely declared than by Paul in his letter to the Corinthians (2 Corinthians 3:4-end). A somewhat obscure argument concludes with the glorious affirmation that we are being changed by the Lord who is Spirit, from one degree of glory to another. No veil on our faces or on our hearts hides the glory of God from us. We can see it when Christ is preached to us, when we read of him in scripture, and when we meet with him in the Eucharist.

It is when we see that glory, and Christ who is the fullest expression of it, that we ourselves are changed. To some extent, change takes place through our daily contact with other people. For better or for worse, for richer or for poorer, they leave their mark upon us. The stronger their personality the more significant is the imprint which they leave upon us. How much more therefore the impact and influence of the risen Christ! Just as we cannot save ourselves, so we cannot change ourselves into his likeness. Only the power of the risen Lord can do that.

Today's Gospel readings in the Eucharist take us to the heart of the matter. Here majesty and suffering, death and glory walk hand in hand. Our Lord is indeed revealed in glory, but it is within the context of his death or 'departure'. The very subject which the disciples repudiated at Caesarea Philippi now becomes the topic of conversation between this amazing threesome in glory. Thus the cross finds its true perspective.

Who can blame the privileged disciples for wanting to prolong such an experience? Have we not all attempted to keep hold of some of those special unveilings of God's glory which come our way from time to time? To be with Christ in glory, is not this the ultimate desire of us all? But there can be no glorying in the presence of Jesus apart from the conflicts of the mission of Jesus. As Michael Ramsey was so fond of reminding us, it was the whole Christ who was transfigured. He carried the conflicts up the mountain so that they could be transfigured with him. That is also why he descended to the valley, for there were people down there to be transformed and conflicts to be transfigured as well.

Our Lord comes to his church in word and sacrament, and we behold him in glory. But he also awaits his church in the poor — the powerless, voiceless and choiceless, where we behold him in brokenness — but where his transforming power can enable his glory to be seen in the most unlikely people and the most unpromising situations.

Fifth Sunday
of Lent

The King and the Kingdom:
The Victory of the Cross

Michael Townsend

OUR instinctive reaction when we are hurt or attacked, is to lash out: 'They are not going to get away with that!' we say. We fight for our dignity and freedom. Yet, strangely, at the heart of one of the gospels for today (Mark 10:32-45) is Jesus who prepares to submit himself to the hurt, indignity, injustice, cruelty and pain of crucifixion in a quite different way. Even more strangely, as we read the gospel narrative we realise that although Jesus was the victim, he was also free. Somehow, he was in charge. He submitted himself to be bound, scourged, tried, mocked and crucified, but he had great dignity and self-control. When, later, he said to Pontius Pilate, 'You would have no power over me if it were not given to you from above' (John 19:11), we realise that he spoke the literal truth. Jesus the victim was free in ways we almost never experience. In situations of stress most of us react as a bundle of barely-understood complexes. Anger, guilt, resentment and sadness within us, battle it out. We cannot remain passive, but scarcely know what to do. Jesus, however, knew exactly who, and what, he was. He knew the security of the Father's love enfolding him and the call of God which came to him. Because he was so secure in these ways, he was inwardly free. Thus there was nothing which could ultimately hurt or destroy him. With great dignity and control he let evil have its way, knowing to whom the eventual victory would belong.

One of today's other readings (Hebrews 9:11-14) is difficult for us, moving in a world of religious experience which is no longer ours. We have never supposed that the blood of goats and bull calves could do anything for us in the sight of God, and find it difficult to understand how anybody might ever have thought that it could. It would be a pity if we missed the important contrast the writer to the Hebrews wanted to make. He says that the old ways to God brought only the possibility of ritual or formal holiness, whereas the sacrifice of Christ brings an inward change in us and in our relationship with God. Christ can purify our consciences, our inner selves, from dead actions, and thereby set us free to serve the living God. We may never expect to understand this fully, but those who trust in Christ do indeed begin to find that he shares with them his own serenity, his own control, his own utterly undefeatable conviction that if you are God's child, loved by the Father, none of life's injustices, cruelties or evils can bring us to final ruin. Thus, and only thus, can our inner selves which are such breeding grounds of conflict, tension and uncertainty, begin to be purified by the new life Christ brings. That is the way in which we are set free to do our service to the living God.

Palm Sunday

The Foolishness of God

Gordon Roe

ONE of the difficulties about commemorating the same events year after year is that they acquire a certain inevitability. The figure of Jesus moves through the landscape, riding on a donkey, throwing out the money changers, praying with disciples, being beaten and mocked and sent to execution, as if he were passing imperturbably through pre-ordained scenes in a great drama. Even the evangelists themselves (and most of all St. John) give the impression that he is in command of events, even when submissive and silent, consciously completing the divine plan. St. Matthew's eagerness to show how everything that he did was in fulfilment of scripture ('This was to fulfil the prophecy which says, "Tell the daughter of Zion, Here is your king, who comes to you in gentleness, riding on an ass".') confirms the same impression.

Yet, at the beginning of Holy Week, we need especially to recall that Jesus was not just the pivotal character in the divine drama of salvation. As we look back on those events and try to interpret them, we arrange them in a pattern which gives us some inkling of God's intentions (we do that in the collect when we pray to 'Almighty and everlasting God, who in your tender love towards mankind sent your son our Saviour Jesus Christ to take upon him our flesh and to suffer death upon the cross ...'). The point, though, of our insisting on the humanity of Jesus is that at every turn he is faced with choices. There is nothing pre-ordained about his reactions. He is not being manipulated. Moreover, there is nothing pre-ordained about the actions of those around him either. The crowd on Palm Sunday *might* have met him with hostility and indifference, instead of welcoming him and investing his actions with the symbolism of the Feast of Tabernacles: 'You shall take the fruit of citrus trees, palm fronds, and leafy branches and willows from the riverside and you shall rejoice before the Lord your God' (Leviticus 23:40). The money changers might have retaliated. Pilate might have refused to condemn him. Because Jesus acted as he did, and all the other people involved acted as they did, the story came out in a certain way, and we are able to see it as the pattern of our salvation.

But the important thing about our salvation is not its particular pattern, but the fact that it was wrought by a true human being, Jesus, known to us with hindsight as the Son of God, making choices and interacting with the choices of others. That is what Paul points to, when he says that Jews demand signs (the omnipotent God manipulating his creatures), Greeks seek wisdom (discerning a pattern in existence) but we preach Christ crucified (a person acting and being acted upon in conformity with God's will). God risks the world's salvation on the choices of one man, who in turn is at the mercy of other people's choices. The foolishness of God consists of his committing himself utterly to his creation.

Easter Day

∽

A New Way Opened Up

George Carey

Behold I am doing a new thing; now it springs forth do you not see it? (Isaiah 43:19)

EACH of today's readings makes important points about the nature of the new way opened to us.

First, from Isaiah 43:16-21, the new way seems to be a *most unlikely route* — 'I will make a way in the desert'. But this is sometimes the way God takes us in our pilgrimage; through sickness, through suffering; yes, even through the deserts of unbelief and doubt. The cross of Jesus must, surely, have this character. Why did God choose this way? Did Jesus himself have passing doubts about the wisdom of this way? 'My God why hast thou forsaken me?' speaks of passing through a wilderness of desolation that must have been terrifying. And yet, it was a way opened up which has brought us home to God.

Second, John 20:1-10 introduces the new way as a *personal way.* Note the contrasting actions and reactions. Mary could not bring herself to enter the tomb but she alerted others. John first hesitated while Peter went straight in and for him the facts were made apparent. John then followed and *saw* and *believed.* This raises the question for us: the way is open but do we enter, do we see, do we believe? The experience of resurrection is life changing; it changed the disciples' attitudes and way of life. It made them missionaries eager to pave the way for others.

The passage from Revelation 1:10-18 takes us into the very presence of God and to the other side of the cross. It states that the new way is *eternal.* Here is a glimpse of the glory which is Christ's; it is so breathtaking that John is compelled to approximate in his language to the divine beauty. The risen Christ is 'like' a son of man, eyes 'like' a flame of fire, his feet 'like' burnished bronze and his voice 'like' the sound of many waters.

There is something also truly reassuring because John says that the Risen Christ laid his right hand on him and said: 'Fear not, I am the first and the last. I died and behold I am alive for evermore and I have the keys of death and hell'. Here is a wonderful picture that the new way can never be closed because the Risen Christ has the keys; that is, he is in control.

So, on this Easter Day the message rings out from the Christian family that the way is open which has marvellous consequences for us all. It transforms the deserts of our lives; it leads us into the experience of meeting the Risen Christ and secures our future in God.

Little wonder that the theologian John S. Whale wrote: 'The gospels do not explain the resurrection; the resurrection explains the gospels. Belief in the resurrection is not an appendage to the Christian faith; it *is* the Christian faith'.

First Sunday after Easter

The Upper Room

Paul Iles

CHRISTIANS have always had to decide whether Easter is event or interpretation: it is both of course, which raises the further more delicate work of trying to analyse the mix.

In the religious tradition of Jesus and Paul, events were central to meeting with God and developing an understanding of who God is. Judaism has always been concrete rather than speculative. The great song of Moses and the People of God (Exodus 15:1-11) unambiguously celebrates an event. Pharoah was defeated and God's People found freedom of a new kind in a new environment. Some will want to take the reported details of that historical event as interpretation. Nevertheless, this Jewish song celebrates a fact, and in doing so proclaims God — in his uniqueness, his holiness and his glorious deeds.

The same God, in the fulness of time, raised Jesus from death to life; again demonstrating that he achieves his purposes through events and what the psalmist calls 'marvellous works'. Another passage for today, (1 Peter 1:3-9) is a Christian song (to complement the Jewish song) of praise to God who continues to reveal his character in his deeds; and, adds the author, 'this is cause for great joy', offering us 'living hope' and an inheritance which 'nothing can destroy or spoil or wither'.

In the Fourth Gospel (John 20:19-29), Jesus brings the disciples to the source of this unending joy. They are drawn deeper into knowledge of the Father, and then through the Son they also receive his unique gift of peace. A gift, which like the resurrection itself, bursts the boundaries of known experience because it is not 'of this world' (Jesus had already said to them, 'Peace I leave with you; my peace I give to you; not as the world gives do I give to you' John 14:27).

The 'other-worldly' quality of the resurrection event and experience demands a particular way of 'seeing and believing',

71

which Thomas only slowly and painfully discovers. There can be no absolute and certain method for discovering the Risen Christ. Each believer comes to faith in their risen Lord by his or her own route. Thomas through doubt; John when he joined Peter in the empty tomb; then Peter, even though hurrying after John he was the first to go into the tomb; others, when they came 'to know the scriptures'; yet more, when they recognised Jesus in the breaking of bread.

On both occasions when the disciples met in the Upper Room, they were afraid and secured the doors against intruders. Now, by contrast, those who live in the power of the risen Lord need have no fear. They can open the doors and take their faith out into the world and live it to the full.

First Sunday
after Easter

The Bread of Life

Paul Iles

BREAD is often called 'the staff of life', meaning that, like
a wooden staff, it is a support to the weak. But bread is also
a basic requirement for survival for the whole human race, strong
or weak. However, today's readings go beyond our need of food
and raise the question, 'what else is basic for survival?' and gives
the answer — God's presence and power.

An Old Testament passage (Exodus 16:2-15) tells how, having
left the security they had known in Egypt, the Israelites confront
these basic needs — perhaps for the first time in such a painful
way. Their complaint is hunger, and it is lodged against Moses.
But that proves to be a mistake. They have mistaken the physical
for the spiritual: a common enough failing. The Jews have
misunderstood their real need and misdirected their complaint.
Moses has to teach them that the privation they face in the
wilderness is not their capacity for survival but their poverty of
spirit, their lack of faith in God and their inability to discern his
ways.

Hunger is comparatively easily satisfied, even in the desert,
though in a strange and unexpected way. The perception of God,
however, is not so easily developed in such harsh surroundings.
Moses and Aaron promise that the people will see 'the glory of
the Lord' as clearly here in the desert as ever before. For the
wilderness experience is about finding God and putting trust in
him. In the Old Testament, hunger satisfied is always a sign of
God's presence: and wherever God is, there his glory can be seen.

A New Testament passage (1 Corinthians 15:53-end) moves on
from the spiritual foundations for life in this world (the presence
of God) to the further question — what happens at death? Does
that experience of total collapse and extinction remove the presence
of God from us or not? The Bible calls death 'the last enemy'.
It is the final point of struggle, between God's creative power

to give life, and the opposing forces of destruction which try to rob humanity of both life and the Life-giver. 'But', says St. Paul, 'God be praised, he gives us the victory through our Lord Jesus Christ'. Because of Christ, neither our wilderness experiences nor even death contain within them any power of final destruction. We can be assured of God's presence 'in this world and the next'.

In one of the gospels (John 6:32-40) Jesus reveals the unshakeable basis for this hope and trust in God. He teaches all his friends to ask the Father for bread — our daily bread — which, as prefigured in the Old Testament experience, continues to provide us with the sustenance of his abiding presence. For the Christian, daily bread is the eucharistic bread, nothing less than Jesus himself ('the true bread which comes down from heaven'), and through it we have the greatest of all the signs of God's presence — his resurrection-power at work in Christ.

So the daily bread which Jesus gives is the life of the Kingdom which is coming; and it sustains us through good and ill, through this passing age and on into the eternal life of the Age to Come. When we accept the crucified Lord as the final and irreversible sign of the presence of God among us, then already we taste heaven, the place where God is for ever. No wonder we pray, 'give us *this bread* always'.

Second Sunday
after Easter

The Good Shepherd

Paul Iles

'IF you want a job done properly — do it yourself' we sometimes say. One of the Old Testament passages (Ezra 34:7-16) shows the exasperation of God with those who had been entrusted with the task of caring for his people, the shepherds of Israel. With anger, God takes the task back into his own hands. In a passage as beautiful as the famous 23rd psalm, he says, 'I myself will tend my flock, I myself pen them in their fold, I will search for the lost, recover the straggler, bandage the hurt, strengthen the sick, leave the healthy and strong to play, and give them their proper food'.

Shepherding is never a romantic or sentimental job, as anyone who has done it will testify. Ezekiel probably had the typical town-dweller's idealised view of shepherding and the countryside. He is using a well-tried and familiar pastoral image to speak of a well-ordered society with a caring community among its citizens, which he believes is God's intention for his people. The order of priorities is significant. Caring depends on order to be fully effective. The divine activity is rule, before it can be rescue and care.

In a New Testament passage (1 Peter 5:1-11) the long established image of the shepherd as ruler and pastor is now applied to the leaders of the Christian community. Peter speaks from experience, as a 'fellow-elder'. They have to exercise care and service among 'the flock of God', which surely means the Christian community and which should itself be well-ordered and caring if it is to be a healthy group.

Rescue, this time, is not from irresponsible 'shepherds' but from our principal adversary — the 'devil'; an incarnation of all that is evil, all the destructive forces which try to pull down what God labours so lovingly, painstakingly and unendingly to establish and build up. But St. Peter's words should also be applied to the role of the Church in its duties to Society. Christian ministry is not limited to the Church. It must not be a selfish activity but put at the disposal of the world.

One of the gospels (John 10:7-16) pursues another traditional contrast, which the prophets of Israel had drawn, between true and false shepherds. Jesus calls them the good shepherd and the hireling. First he warns against the hireling, the false shepherd, or indeed the false prophet. Then he describes himself as the good shepherd and points out the difference between the good and the false. Ownership is the clue. Between the hireling and his sheep there is a distance and lack of care because 'the sheep are not his'. Whereas the good shepherd counts his sheep, knows them by name and enjoys with them a relationship based on belonging to one another.

From the very beginning, biblical religion taught that the relationship between God and his people (called the covenant-relationship) expresses the intimate knowledge of the One with the other. The same strong link binds Master and disciples: Jesus and those he calls his friends. Such links of intimacy are unbreakable. Therefore Jesus is one who lays down his life for his friends. The cross and resurrection demonstrate the extent of the Father's love for us, which in turn binds all together. The unity of the flock grows out of the single-mindedness of the shepherd rather than any desire of the sheep to stick together.

Second Sunday
after Easter

The Emmaus Road

Paul Iles

THE Pilgrim's Way stretches from Winchester to Canterbury,
or from England to Compostella in Spain, or from Jerusalem
to Emmaus, or indeed from earth to heaven. To be a pilgrim has
always been a powerful image of the Christian life. Pilgrims travel
together — which always provides an opportunity for a particular
kind of growth in the individual and the group. To company with
another means literally to be sharing bread together, and intimacy
at this level can lead to much deepening understanding and
growing trust and affection between people.

An incident in the New Testament, (Luke 24:13-35) is an
example — two broken men with 'faces downcast' walk towards
Emmaus and are joined by a third. They tell the stranger who
comes alongside them what they have been discussing — the
collapse of all their hopes, both religious and national, sacred and
secular. They speak of Jesus and his death, adding that they had
hoped he would be 'the one to set Israel free'. In a conversation
among Jews, that phrase meant one thing — Messiah — the one
anointed by God and equipped by him to bring in his Kingdom.
The pilgrims had believed Jesus might have been nothing less
than God's Messiah who would bring in the long awaited 'Last
Days' and the everlasting Kingdom.

Throughout the Bible the metaphor of God's Kingdom and
sovereign rule is used to state and define the relationship between
God and his creation. Jews believe that God is not only originator
of the world but also sovereign over it. What is more his rule
is effective: challenged, threatened, at times eclipsed, but
ultimately sovereign.

Not only Jews could look to the Kingdom in hope, but all
humanity. In one of today's readings (Isaiah 25:6-9), Isaiah's
vision is of what happens in the coming Kingdom. 'All the
peoples' will enjoy a feast provided by the Lord on the
mountaintop'.

The experience of the Jews, however, proved that fulfilment only comes through periods of waiting, indeed of exile and rejection. But they had reason to believe God could be trusted. They had walked the Way of the Lord before, and knew. So the visionary sings of God and the time to come: 'This is the Lord for whom we have waited: let us rejoice and exult in his deliverance'.

Another vision, from the New Testament (Revelation 19:6-9), picks up the same theme. It describes the sound of a vast crowd — surely another way of saying 'all the peoples' — singing praise to God 'who has entered on his sovereign reign'. Those who first heard this poem believed Jesus' death and resurrection was the moment of that entrance upon sovereignty.

What perplexed the two pilgrims was that for them the crucifixion of Jesus declared he could *not* be Messiah. He had not only been rejected by his people but also allowed by God to die without rescue. Before they could re-shape this central part of their creed, they had to re-interpret their scriptures. Their companion helped them, and raised in their minds a new question — 'was it not ordained that the Christ should suffer and so enter into his glory?' Once they could glimpse the Kingdom in this new way, as fulfilment, then they could accept a crucified Messiah; they could see how victory might come out of defeat; and how the 'now but not yet' tension between time and eternity is resolved within the Kingdom.

Third Sunday
after Easter

The Lakeside

Paul Iles

HOME-thoughts from abroad moved Robert Browning and he shared his vision with us in an unforgettable poem. The prophet in exile dreams of a time of restoration and fresh beginnings in his ancient homeland (Isaiah 61:1-7). When 'the year of the Lord's favour' comes, there will be a dramatic transformation — 'garlands instead of ashes, oil of gladness instead of mourner's tears'; and a reversal from the double measure of jeers and insults to a double measure of wealth and everlasting joy. God always gives good measure, pressed down and running over: 'more than either we desire or deserve'.

But such a transformation comes about only through the presence and power of God and his servant — 'the one upon whom his Spirit rests'. The prophet spoke of this transformation in terms of his nation's life. St. Paul knew a transformation within himself (1 Corinthians 15:1-11). Since the appearance to him of the Risen Christ on the Damascus Road (his abnormal birth as an apostle), his life had been transformed. Not through his own efforts, though, although he can say he has worked more strenuously than others, but through God's grace. 'By God's grace I am what I am', became as it were his personal motto.

In one of the gospels (John 21:1-14), transformation and the filling of human emptiness by a divine presence and power are the clues needed to understand the mysterious appearance of Jesus to his disciples — this time in Galilee rather than Jerusalem. The disciples are in need — they have toiled all night and caught nothing. They are hungry, and apparently have made no provision for breakfast. Once they see and recognise Jesus their nothingness is transformed into abundance and their hunger is met; and he provides the meal they need to sustain them.

This incident from the working life of a group of fishermen reveals much more. It illuminates Jesus' promise that he would

79

make his disciples (and now the Church) agents of mission, 'fishers of men'. Significantly this work of mission is always based on the principles already enunciated — it is not done in human strength but through God, and the starting point is always human emptiness not human achievements. But once the presence of the Lord is recognised within that emptiness, then the result is assured and a real and lasting transformation can come.

Mission is a command laid upon all Jesus' friends in every generation. 'Let down your net' each of us is told. When we undertake this task, however daunting and impossible it seems, we find ourselves in touch with a transforming power, our needs are met and our prayers answered. When St. Paul heard and heeded Jesus' voice he became the apostle to the Gentiles and discovered 'If any man be in Christ, he is a new creature'. That transformation became the basis of his confidence in God's power to restore his broken people and establish his Kingdom among them.

Third Sunday
after Easter

The Resurrection and the Life

Paul Iles

ONE approach to the Bible, particularly popular in the Middle Ages, is to look for parallels between events in the two Testaments — the Old and the New. For instance, many schemes of iconography used in stained glass windows are designed in pairs; as the windows in King's College Chapel, Cambridge show. The same thing happens in two of today's readings in a remarkable way, and they complement each other in many details (1 Kings 17:17-end; John 11:17-27).

Elijah is asked by the widow of Zarephath to restore her son to life. The two sisters Martha and Mary turn to Jesus in their need and longing for him to restore their brother Lazarus to life.

Both accounts start with resentment. The widow blames Elijah for her child's death. Martha said to Jesus, 'If you had been here, my brother would not have died'. Elijah prays before his action and makes no particular claim for himself. But Jesus invites faith and belief from the sisters, and another of the Johannine great affirmations is voiced — 'I am the resurrection and the Life'.

Neither miracle of raising to life-again is done for sensational effect but after a deep and passionate request and each reveals the credibility of the man of God — Elijah and Jesus. 'Now I know you are a man of God and that the Lord really speaks through you', says the widow. 'I now believe you are the Messiah the Son of God who was to come into the world', says Martha.

These two events remind us that among God's promises to his people is the gift of new-life, life-restored, a foretaste of life beyond death. The Old Testament spells out who would be the agent who brings about the fulfilment of this promise: either one of the prophets of the Kingdom or the Messiah.

A prophet (deutero-Isaiah) had said God's chosen servant would, 'bring captives out of prison, out of the dungeons where they now lie in darkness'. For a Jew this meant release from sheol, the place where departed spirits inhabited a kind of limbo, waiting for the final acts of divine creation to bring them either to fulfilment or extinction.

Elijah, particularly, was regarded as 'the prophet of the Kingdom' and Jesus knew himself to be 'Messiah', anointed and equipped by God to bring in the resurrection. The widow's son and Lazarus are brought out of the prison-house and set free because they are participating in the coming of the Kingdom of God.

Elijah's status is a prophet; Jesus is at least 'among the prophets' but he goes further and incarnates the Kingdom, and the ways of bringing in that Kingdom, in himself. He himself goes to the cross and opens up the path to resurrection-life. He is 'the resurrection and the life' and all who, in Paul's words, are 'in Christ' participate in the explosive power of healing and restoration which his death and resurrection release into the world.

Fourth Sunday after Easter

The Charge to Peter

Paul Iles

WHAT'S in a name? Certainly some mysterious power — which is why in scripture so much importance is attached to names. A name is more than a means of identification: it gives a strong indication of character. Jesus deliberately re-named Simon the fisherman and called him Peter, pointing to the character he intended for this particular disciple.

But a change of heart and a change of character are never simple and immediate. Such transformations are only possible through the powerful, creative work of God. He alone (according to today's Collect) can bring order to the unruly wills and passions of sinful men; a creative process which is indeed powerful but inevitably also painful, demanding and costly.

One of today's readings (Isaiah 62:1-5) is about such a change, but in a nation rather than in individual. It describes the time when Israel went into exile and her reputation, her standing among the nations, and her beauty were eclipsed. The prophet promises that she will be transformed and vindicated — publicly, openly, and all will see that 'the Lord's delight' is in her. 'As the bridegroom rejoices over the bride so shall God rejoice over you'. Through the creative power of God, a new character replaces a former one and Israel is given a new name — the bride.

New life is the continuing promise of the risen Lord to all who believe the Gospel. Such new life however can only be gift, not earned, and in a New Testament passage (Revelation 3:14-end) we hear how Jesus stands at the door and knocks. Only those prepared to open the door to him can receive the gift he longs to give. There is also the warning: 'Those whom I love, I reprove and chasten'. Those who look for renewal must accept the demands of the process. The lack-lustre church of Laodicea needed to be changed through the vigorous and painful judgement of God. If they are to be granted God's will and become

83

conquerors, they are charged to 'be zealous and repent'.

In one of today's gospels (John 21:15-22) Jesus first addresses Peter by his old name — Simon. It's as though nothing had happened since his first meeting with Jesus and the first days of his discipleship. It was almost too much for Peter to bear. His former impetuousity begins to burst out again. He was grieved that Jesus treated him in this way. Yet he couldn't side-step the need for forgiveness and healing after his terrible words of denial. Peter may not have realised it at once, but Jesus had no option. Because he loved Peter and wanted him to be a foundation pillar of the Church, he must chasten him. Peter underwent the painful process of renewal, but from it emerged his new enlarged task given by Jesus — the task of leadership and pastoral care — feed my lambs, tend my sheep. By being obedient to this call to work, restoration came to Peter and his old energy was renewed and re-directed.

In baptism we are baptised into the name of Jesus (1 Corinthians 1:13,15). This is symbolised by the name we receive, a Christian name. Baptism gives us membership of the Church, but at the same time we are charged with a task — we are commissioned to take our share in the ministry of the People of God. Like Simon, we receive a new name, indicative of what we are meant to be, and called to accept the costly path of renewal and self-giving. If we go this way, we shall find even our unruly wills and passions being changed by God.

Fourth Sunday
after Easter

The Way, the Truth
and the Life

Paul Iles

PROVERBS and well-known sayings stick in the memory to provide comfort and correction. We draw them out like postcards from time to time to re-call our beliefs; or use them as a compass to re-set the direction of our pilgrimage.

The book of scripture called *Proberbs* was carefully gathered and composed because the writer believed the wisdom contained in its brief sayings was essential for life with God. In one of today's readings (Proverbs 4: 10-19) he contrasts two ways of life — the way of the wicked, which is like deep darkness, and the path of the righteous, which is like the light of dawn. Those who desire to be with God must choose between them, for only *one* way can lead to truth and life.

The contrast between the darkness and light which surround the two possible paths echoes a creation myth in Genesis. The spirit of God brooded on the face of the waters which represented the deep darkness of chaos out of which God fashioned his creation. When God said, 'let there be light', there was light.

For those who choose the better way — the way of the righteous — long life is the reward and while there is freedom of pace ('when you walk, your step will not be hampered, and if you run, you will not stumble'), the wise man must keep close to his guide (the instructor of wisdom) and discipline himself to make sure he keeps to the right path. For even if we set out on the right path with determination and deliberation, we shall be tempted to wander from it and need to be recalled to it over and over again.

One of the New Testament passages (2 Corinthians 4:13-5:5) begins with another contrast: between the outward body, which is in decay, and the inward body, which is being renewed daily. Those who have chosen the way of the righteous, and who seek the truth, can expect their life to be a process of being sifted and renewed daily. Our mortal nature is being absorbed into life immortal. This can be a frightening and disburbing process. To sustain us through such a test of faith, St. Paul (our guide this time) urges us to fix our eyes, 'not on the things that are seen, but on the things which are unseen' — for these are the things which endure and provide the only truth worth knowing.

In one of the gospels (John 14:1-11) there is a fuller discussion of the journey to the Father which the Christian is making and the path along which he travels. Thomas, the man with doubts and the one who is always prepared to speak bluntly and push his point, says to Jesus, 'Lord we do not know where you are going, so how can we know the way?' This prompts another of the great affirmations of the Christ in the Fourth Gospel — 'I am the way, I am the truth and I am life; no one comes to the Father except by me'.

Like the disciples, the cause of much human anxiety is still that we do not feel sure we know the way Jesus is going. But he can set our troubled hearts at rest, because now the journey and the goal are one: brought together in the person of Jesus. He is our companion along the way. He is our guide who brings us into touch with the Spirit who leads us into all truth. He is the source of all life, whether it is the gift of creation, or life abundant, which is the gift of the Spirit, or resurrection-life, which is God's final gift to his people.

So to be with Jesus is already to be with the Father and Jesus promises his friends that in any further journeying which needs to be taken, he will come to us himself and bring us to God. The early Church lived with this hope and expectation and prayed earnestly 'Even so, come Lord Jesus, come'. Every generation of Christian people makes that prayer their own.

Fifth Sunday
after Easter

Going to the Father

Neville Clark

SEPARATION is a reality constituting one of the major threats to human well-being. At the same time, it provides the indispensable condition for personal growth and maturity. If a mother leaves her baby, anxiety ensues, loss pervades, insecurity floods in, forsakenness fills all horizons, survival feels put at risk. Yet, unless a mother leaves her baby, identity is strangled at birth, growth is scuppered, personal integration is stifled, relationship is prohibited from emergence. The resolution of this impasse is 'return'. Going gives place again to coming; sorrow to joy. An impossible, unthinkable, double-sided promise is proved true. 'A little while, and you will not see me, and again a little while, and you will see me.'

This is the rhythm of all subsequent life. Separation threatens, and may scar. Separation spurs, and may bear personal fruit. Return reassures, and may heal. Return authenticates faithfulness, and turns sorrow into joy. In some strange fashion, the intensity of the joy reflects the density of the sorrow.

Death menaces precisely because it heralds ultimate separation. The identity of the self seems set at risk in face of the return of the body to the earth whence it came. Others, who have shared in the intimacy of the profound rhythm of goings and comings that define relationship, face the agony of a going that carries no certificate of return. So it is that the faithful rhythm of life stands locked in conflict with the contradictory finality of terminus that death provides. Who or what will arbitrate and designate the victor?

Into this scenario, the Gospel of John drops a dress-rehearsal. A separation is foreshadowed. A death is signalled. A return is certified. A compass-bearing clue is tabled: 'because I go to the Father' (John 16:12-24). Perhaps this is more than a road map of a journey of Jesus. Perhaps it signals a re-routing of all our human relationships. To go to the Father is to be where Jesus belongs. Yet because he is Way, Truth, Life, the ground on which we make our human pilgrimages, the reality which undergirds us, the secret heart of all our living, it is also where *we* now belong. He 'goes' in order that the Spirit may 'come'. The Christ of the Galilean road returns as the Lord of every road. Into the mutual belonging of Father, Son, and Spirit, disciples are drawn. Because Jesus goes away, and because it is to the Father that he goes, and because it is through the Spirit that he returns, disciples — and we — are drawn into a network of reunion that death cannot sever.

Once, a nation lost its Moses, found him replaced by a Joshua, and inherited a Promised Land (Deuteronomy 34). Now, neither death nor life nor you name it will be able to separate us from the love of God in Christ Jesus our Lord (Romans 8:28-39). The experience of separation remains. It is part both of our human brokenness and of the necessary rhythm of our road to maturity. But the labour pains of anguish are the herald of the joy of new life.

Sunday after Ascension

The Ascension

Gordon Mursell

IN Dostoyevsky's great novel *The Brothers Karamazov*, the Grand Inquisitor asks Jesus why he has chosen to reappear in the world, in Spain at the time of the Inquisition. 'Why did you come to meddle with us?' he asks. He reminds Jesus that he had handed over all authority to the church before his Ascension. 'So,' he goes on , 'there's no need for you to come at all now; and, at any rate, do not interfere.'

The Grand Inquisitor's words are a recurrent temptation for Christians, and they serve to underline the crucial importance of the Ascension. Before it, Christ's presence was limited to a particular place and people at a particular time. After it, his presence became universal. A limited Christ is much easier to cope with, and generations of Christians have found it irresistibly tempting to apply fresh limits to replace the old ones; in other words, to keep Christ locked up, a prisoner of their particular ideology or prejudice a mascot to be wheeled out under strict ecclesiastical control in order to justify or canonize the prevailing fashion or sectarian cause.

But Christ is not the property of the church. The church is the property of Christ. And it has no monopoly of his presence, or of the Holy Spirit that was his gift. The reason is the story of the Ascension. Jesus did not tell his disciples to go straight out and convert the world. He told them to 'stay in the city until you are clothed with the power from on high' (Luke 24:45-end). Once Christ had ascended, the disciples had to sit still and wait for the free gift of his Spirit. It came, as and when it chose. Only then were the disciples empowered to go out into the world. And, from that day onwards, Christians did not just *bring* Christ to the world. They *found* Christ in the world, his presence constantly widening ecclesiastical horizons and defying ecclesiastical control. That is what St. Paul means when he writes 'the Church is Christ's body, the completion of him who himself completes all things everywhere' (Ephesians 1:15-end). Christians do not make Christ *present*. They do not have to. They do have to make Christ *known*.

And there's an even more important point still. Earlier in his letter to the Ephesians, St. Paul says that 'the word "ascended" implies that (Christ) also descended to the lowest level, down to the very earth' (Ephesians 4:1-13). The language and imagery may sound foreign today. But the meaning is crucial. After the Ascension, there is no part of creation, from the depths to the heights, that are cut off from the presence of the risen Christ. Christ ascended *and descended*. The darkest dimensions of human life and experience, as well as the highest ones, are known to him. The earth itself, and its fragile and constantly threatened fruitfulness, is holy. The reason the first disciples 'were continually in the Temple praising God' (Luke 24:45-end) was because they knew what we easily forget: that Christ's Ascension did not mean his departure. It meant, precisely, his arrival, and the assurance of his presence, in every part of the creation. From then on, even Grand Inquisitors were not immune from his challenge, or excluded from his love.

Pentecost Sunday

∼

'Come, Holy Spirit'

Perpetua Towell, OSB

THE readings for the feast of Pentecost are full of contrasts. When men had one language they used it to make a name for themselves. On the day of Pentecost there were many languages but one theme: the mighty works of God. On Sinai God came down in fire and smoke and the people dared not approach the mountain. In the upper room tongues of fire rested on the heads of the apostles, not to burn but to illuminate, not to destroy but to enlighten. In the Gospels we hear Jesus saying to those he is leaving that he will come back to them. Through the Spirit, whom the Father will send to them, they will know the truth: know the relationship of Jesus with his Father; know that the Father loves them, know that together they will come and make their home with those who love the Son and keep his word.

Wind and fire, love poured into our hearts like water on soil that is parched and cracked: symbols of the Spirit at work within us, 'hiddenly, secretly, like leaven working heaven'. Yet Archbishop William Temple warned that when we say, 'Come, Holy Ghost, our souls inspire', we had better know what we are about. 'If we invoke him it will be to do God's will, not ours. We cannot call upon him to use omnipotence for the supply of our futile pleasures or the success of our futile plans. If we invoke him we must be ready for the glorious pain of being caught by his power out of our petty orbit into the eternal purposes of the Almighty.'

Mark Frank, Prebendary and Treasurer of St. Paul's in the seventeenth century, also reminds us that no place is exempt from the wind of the Spirit: 'It finds St. Matthew at the receipt of custom and blows him out of a publican into an Apostle. It blows St. Peter and St. Andrew out of their boat to the stern of the Church of Christ ... No place so remote but it can reach; none so private that it can find; none so strong but it can break through; ... and none so bad, but some way or other it will vouchsafe to visit.'

We are to be witnesses to this power of the Spirit. We may not have to proclaim our faith in words, but we cannot flee from what we are: witnesses by our lives to God's mighty works. We are to be witnesses to his marvellous work of creation when at the first the Spirit moved over the primeval chaos, a creation which is now in danger from our selfish and reckless exploitation of the earth's resources. We are to be witnesses to the yet more wonderful work of God's new creation in the Incarnation as we see in Jesus the Spirit at work in our humanity, showing us what we can be like in terms of self-giving love. We are to be witnesses to that love in so far as, open to the Spirit, we are ready to be changed into loving people. 'See how these Christians love one another' was first said, not in sarcasm as so often today, but as the truth.

On the evening of the first Easter day, the risen Lord breathed on his disciples and said: 'Receive Holy Spirit'. He gave them the power of forgiveness, a power to set men free, to heal them. We are witnessing today a renewal of the healing ministry of the Church. Sometimes there will be dramatic signs of the Spirit at work to heal, but he also works gently in the hidden recesses of the heart to bring peace, shalom, which is wholeness in the fullest sense.

Come, Holy Spirit, and kindle in us the fire of your love.

Trinity Sunday

The Glory of God

Andrew Naylor

ISAIAH of Jerusalem was not the sort of person who would feel comfortable having afternoon tea at the Vicarage! He has been variously described and depicted as a bit of a rough and ready customer, who was not afraid to speak out when the 'big' people in society were ignoring or, even worse, picking-off the 'little' people. His message to the people of Israel was one of justice for the poor, and a rebuke to those who were engaged in the motions of ritual worship, but ignored the plight of the hungry and the homeless. There was nothing genteel about him. It might, therefore, come as a bit of a surprise to find him in one of todays readings (Isaiah 6:1-8) in the temple at Jerusalem, experiencing the presence of God and all the heavenly hosts and the choirs of angels. Surely this is a bit out of context?

Isaiah's call, an experience common to the prophets, marks the start of his public ministry. It happened with Jesus at his baptism, when the majestic holiness of the Father's voice was heard from heaven. But Isaiah is overcome by the experience, and offers a very strong argument as to why he should not be a prophet — 'I am unworthy'. But the purposes of God cannot be hindered by human unworthiness! There is a mission to be fulfilled, and, true to the old cliché, God chooses some of the most unexpected people, because it is they who will help to fulfil his purposes.

The experience of Isaiah points to one essential truth: the Trinity is not a cold theological concept which is discussed in seminar rooms in universities, it is a living reality in the world. That is why God's holiness in the temple, and Isaiah's mission among the poor, the orphaned, and the hungry are so inseparable. God's holiness, his care for humanity, and his involvement in life are all bound-up together.

Another of today's readings states this truth in explicitly Christian terms (Ephesians 1:3-14). The Father of Jesus, the God of Abraham, Isaac and Jacob, the God of Isaiah's vision, is the God who got involved in the world *in* Jesus. He shared our common humanity, disclosed to us his purposes, and brought us 'into unity in Christ'. And, even now, we are being daily strengthened by the presence of his spirit, which is a pledge of our sharing in his life.

You cannot separate God's holiness from his down-to-earthness, any more than you can separate the unity of Father, Son and Holy Spirit. For to know God, is to have seen something of his activity in the world, in our worship, and the lives of others. His presence is constant, it is even surprising.

Second Sunday of Pentecost

≈

The People of God

Perpetua Towell OSB

TODAY'S theme focuses our attention upon the vocation of the People of God and the collect, in the fewest possible words, gives us a whole theology of what it means. Vocation is a word out of fashion today, replaced by career, which, according to the *Shorter Oxford Dictionary*, means a profession providing opportunities for advancement. Vocation implies a call, an invitation to which we respond; for the Christian it is a call from God and it is to him we make our response. It begins in baptism; it grows out of baptism, for we have been baptised into one body, a phrase rich in meaning. It signifies the Church, the mystical body of Christ into which we are incorporated; his body broken on the cross and offered to us the Eucharist; his body recognised or rejected as we discern or fail to discern him in every other human being.

The great Belgian liturgist, Abbot Capelle, once wrote: 'Strictly speaking, for the Christian, there are no individuals but only members.' It is this which distinguishes a vocation from a career if we accept the dictionary's definition. We are not aiming at advance up the ladder for ourselves but trying to serve God to the glory of his name. Within the Church there will be a variety of ministries, all equally God's gift and needed. We are reminded of St. Paul's parable of the physical body: no one member can detach itself from the rest saying it has no need of them. The intimate call of God has to be worked out through interaction with others. It may be heard suddenly, dramatically as for Paul on the Damascus Road, or gradually, even evaded for a time. God does not call once and then leave us; his bidding is his enabling.

However varied, however different the circumstances in which it has to be lived out, the essence of every vocation is the service of God in holiness and truth. A strange pair to be juxtaposed. St. Benedict recognised the danger lurking in the pursuit of holiness unallied to truth. One of the tools of the spiritual craft with which he provides his monks is 'Not to wish to be called holy before one is that one may be so called the more truly.' We need the humility which is truth, recognising our strengths and our weaknesses and handing them over to the Spirit, who sanctifies not only the Body in its totality, but every member of it.

In some of the readings there is the same insistence on vocation being a gift of God and the same call to holiness as its essence. Moses is to remind the people of Israel that their escape from Egypt was God's doing: 'I bore you on eagle's wings' (Exodus 19:1-6). If they respond they will be his own possession, a holy nation. The reading from 1 Peter, possibly part of a homily to the newly baptised, declares that what was promised but never fulfilled is now accomplished in Christ. We have been brought out of darkness into light, made a spiritual temple, a holy priesthood, God's own people (1 Peter 2:1-10). In the Gospel we are shown how this is possible. As the sap rises and flows through every branch of the vine making it alive and fruitful, so if we remain, make our home in Jesus and allow him to make his home with us, our fruit bearing will be abundant (John 15:1-5). If we cut ourselves off, we are useless.

Another group of readings have the same theme. The Old Testament reading speaks of God's choice of David and the promise that his house will be established for ever (2 Samuel 7:4-16). The prophecy was fulfilled in a very different King: Jesus rejected by his own people and his throne a cross. The promise remains and by baptisms we are brought into the Kingdom, sharing the common life, the sacraments, the worship and the teaching of the apostles.

The parables of Jesus are often meant to shock and surprise us. Can God really be like the man who gives the big dinner party? Yes, this is what his love is like, when it is refused it can explode, for anger is the other side of love; any other alternative would be indifference. God's love invites us, wants us to come into his house, wants us to be happy; but we *can* refuse.

Third Sunday
after Pentecost

The Life of the Baptised

Timothy Jenkins

THE people of God are created by God's acts and live in the light of his promise, that he will complete what he has begun. Yet their history, collectively and individually, is marked by repeated failure to live in accordance with the character of God, as revealed in those acts and that promise. There is a tension between the status that God has given and the business of living up to that status, a distinction upon which today's readings reflect.

This tension haunts those who are baptised, perhaps particularly those of us baptised as children. On the one hand, we are full members of the Church by virtue of our baptism. And yet on the other hand, most of us do not feel we live up to the promise of our baptism: we live largely unredeemed lives. Being a member is both a matter of status and of potential, and the passage from John (John 15:5-11) emphasizes the importance of fulfilling that potential. Status alone, it is suggested, is not enough; there is the question of what use you make of your status, or how you develop. In this view, baptism is something you grow into, an incomplete, continuing process.

In discussing this process, the Service of Baptism employs the metaphor of the Church being a family, and the parallels are striking. Once a baby is born, he is a full member of the family; but there is still all the question of how he grows and develops. This is a real question for a parent: the process of bringing up a child is not simply a matter of producing another healthy human animal, full of vitality and capable of fulfilling his or her needs and desires, for a child also has the potential to become more than simply a human animal, and to be capable of thinking of others and of showing compassion, care and love. In other words, a human being is not just a clever human animal, but is also a person. And the process of becoming a person is learnt through other people, both in receiving from their generosity and in giving out again.

So the business of becoming human, which begins in the context of the family, involves, on the one hand, a dying to the selfish self and, on the other hand, new life through others. It is an open-ended process, and it bears remarkable resemblances to the business of living out one's baptism.

Indeed, Paul is clear that it is only possible to become human by sharing in the death and new life of Jesus Christ. This is because it would be quite impossible for humans, left to themselves, to fulfil their potential. From all the evidence we have, we appear to have an innate capacity to make a mess of things, to be more animal and less persons. Each human project fails to achieve its ends, each of us suffers from the inattention or wrong attentions of others, and each of us passes on these wrongs to our fellows.

It is only through the work of Jesus Christ, crucified, died and raised from the dead, that it is possible that sin does not have the last word, and that we have the hope, ever renewed, of fulfilling our potential and of becoming fully human.

The life of the baptised is therefore sharing in the death and resurrection of Jesus Christ through faith, dying to our old life and being raised with him into new life. This life is experienced in the mundane business of breaking down and overcoming the patterns of things going badly, in our not passing on the evil we receive, and in others returning good for our evil. It is in these experiences that we live out the potential contained in our membership, and that we find a real ground for our hope.

Fourth Sunday after Pentecost

The Freedom of the Sons of God

Rodney Matthews

THE title must not be allowed to mislead. At first it sounds like *carte-blanche* — 'a blank paper, duly signed, to be filled up at the recipient's pleasure: freedom of action' (*Chambers Dictionary*). But Scripture details the nature of the licence. The emphasis is upon God's choice and the privilege of those who are identified in it.

Whilst in this period of the year the Epistle 'controls' and the other passages support (c.f. *The Calendar and Lectionary*, JLG p. 18), Galatians 3:23-4:7 is not the easiest of Pauline themes to grasp without additional points of reference. The letter is the Apostle's defence of the position of Gentile Christians who, by virtue of their faith and baptism into Christ, are not to be restricted by an outmoded legalistic outlook. Paul then uses Greek and Jewish illustrations. In Greek households a trusted servant was responsible for protecting the child and especially for chaperoning him to school — not to teach but to ensure the child reached his teacher safely. The law, argued Paul, was there to lead a person to Christ and then hand over the charge. The key to freedom from the law was therefore the grace of God in Jesus. A further reference to the growing up process reinforces the point, this time in the Jewish world where, on his twelfth birthday, a boy became 'a son of the law' by which adulthood was conferred and the enjoyment of its privileges. For the Christian that point is reached in Christ.

Reference back to that Deuteronomic world provides a further interpretation of the idea of the control of freedom. It is always within the bounds of the purpose of the Father. The picture in Deuteronomy 7:6-11 is of a family of young children, small, weak and vulnerable, but under the protection of a father who is guardian of his own creative will to provide for the future. God's people have no claim beyond that of enjoying the security of God's pre-determined love. Such a restriction proscribes reckless living but opens the way to true freedom.

And so to the Gospel (John 15:12-17) for the final picture. Jesus is preparing his disciples for a time when they are to be their own men, free to interpret what he has taught them about life. In a classroom of revision he reminds them of the controlling factor: the initiative for their future was his, not theirs. *He* chose *them*, from the shore, the cashdesk, under the figtree, and gave them a new world in which to work out God's purpose for their lives.

That is the freedom of the Christian. The scope is almost limitless. It is the underlying purpose which holds the check: the relationship between father and son binding, so that by the grace of the Lord Jesus Christ the love of God may flow freely into the world through the Christian spirit.

Fifth Sunday after Pentecost

∽

Live in Love

Robert Williamson

BOTH the New Law and the Church's Mission are concerned with life. By endeavouring to fulfil the Old Testament commandments those who did so not only sought to please God, they also desired to find true life. How else can we explain the perplexity surrounding the young man who came to Jesus asking what he must *do* to obtain eternal life. He had kept the Law, or so he claimed, but apparently it had not had the desired effect (Matthew 19:16-26). He lacked that quality of life which he felt should be his. Was this not also the cause of the underlying disappointment which burned within the unconverted Saul of Tarsus? Zealous law-keeping had failed to produce the life of communion with and acceptance by God which he so earnestly sought.

Clearly there was a vital element missing. Not that the Law was faulty but, apparently, it did not go far enough. It wasn't that the Law had to be set aside but, on the contrary, it needed to be fulfilled. The Law is our schoolteacher to bring us to Christ — he is the missing factor. It is Christ who personifies that one element which not only fulfilled the Law but which also gave it its true perspective — namely *love*. It would be mistaken, of course, to imply that love was missing from all Old Testament Law-keeping. There are many glorious instances of love in action, and the story of Ruth and Naomi is a classic example (Ruth 1:8-17,22). The Christian religion does not have a monopoly on love for God and love for our neighbour. Such love is deeply embedded in Judaism, for example, but we believe that it found its perfect expression in the life and teaching of our Lord. Love is the fulfilling of the Law, it doesn't do away with it, but confirms it and provides its correct interpretation.

Love is also to be the supreme characteristic of Christians, the one thing above all else which they must possess if their discipleship in the world is to carry authenticity and power. Love is not one virtue among a list of other virtues, but the sum and substance of what it means to be a Christian. Needless to say this provides today's Christian with no soft option. To 'live in love' as Paul exhorts the Ephesians (Ephesians 5:1-10), is to be committed to 'an unsuspected adventure' — a movement beyond security, comfort and protection, to the risks of love and the demands of service. Pious expressions of love will cut little ice in a divided, broken and suffering world. If we are to be part of God's mission then our love will need to have a practical, genuine and, perhaps, radical feel to it.

That was the kind of love demanded of Peter in the Cornelius incident (Acts 11:4-18). It can really be described as a conversion experience which enabled him to break through the barriers of prejudice and particularity and recognise that God's mission, like God's love, is universal in its scope and application. If it was a conversion experience for Peter, it was nothing less for the Church which, unwittingly, had placed boundaries to the love of God in Christ.

There have always been those within the Church, and they are still with us today, whose main concern has been with *identity* — with survival, safety, solidarity and tradition — and these things are important of course. However, they need to be balanced with a proper concern for *outreach* — risk, openness and vulnerability. It is this second, and perhaps over-riding concern towards which the love and the mission of God calls us. It was in following such a call that the seventy-two launched out on their 'unsuspected adventure' of becoming as lambs in the midst of wolves (Luke 10:1-12). Not the most secure and comfortable of situations but better, surely, to be with God on the risky and adventurous frontiers of mission than languishing in a spiritual lay-by, paralysed by concerns of personal identity and survival.

Sixth Sunday
after Pentecost

❧

The New Man

Timothy Jenkins

THE writer to the Ephesians talks of putting off the old nature and of putting on the new. The difference between the old nature (or man) and the new is that the one is 'alienated from the life of God', because of ignorance due to hardness of heart, while the other is 'renewed in the spirit of his mind ... created after the likeness of God in true righteousness and holiness'.

This distinction echoes something Paul wrote in the letter to the Romans (6:1 ff.): 'You know well enough that if you put yourselves at the disposal of a master, to obey him, you are slaves of the master whom you obey; and this is true whether you serve sin, with death as its result, or obedience, with righteousness as its result'.

The point here is that both the old life and the new life, the old nature and the new, involve our being under one master or another. Neither the new life nor the old life involve us being free from constraint or control. This idea is present in Micah's account of the controversy the Lord has with his people (Micah 6:1-8), and it is fundamental to the Christian perspective: you cannot simply be free, you can only be free from something and free for something. Freedom has to be understood in relation to God, and freedom in Christ is freedom from sin and freedom for righteousness and holiness.

The writer to the Ephesians goes on to elaborate what this freedom might mean in everyday life: the business of telling the truth, not lying, of not letting anger have the last word, of giving to those in need rather than stealing, of putting aside bitterness, malice and angry talk, and instead being kind, tenderhearted and forgiving (Ephesians 4:17-end). Micah is even more succinct: 'What does the Lord require of you (he asks) but to do justice, and to love kindness, and to walk humbly with your God?'.

This sounds straightforward, yet there is a problem, for there is a flaw in human life. We are unable on our own to achieve what seems to lie within our grasp to do; we are continually falling short. It might be put like this: we are, on the whole, free to be who we are, but we are not free to become who we might be, that is, fully human, made in the image of God.

This second freedom is only to be found through God's grace, through God's being with us in Christ. It is through grace, through God's action in us, that we tell the truth rather than lie, that anger does not have the last word, that we give rather than take, show kindness rather than malice, and so forth.

The new man is made by grace. This is the force of the story of Blind Bartimaeus (Mark 10:46-end). He was given faith and persistence, and then was gifted with sight: he was remade. That story concludes: 'At once he recovered his sight and followed (Jesus) on the road'.

Seventh Sunday
after Pentecost

The More Excellent Way

Gordon Roe

IN praying, as we do in the collect, that God will 'pour into our hearts that most excellent gift of love' there is a danger that we shall fasten too strongly onto the word 'hearts'. In our days it suggests feelings, emotions or even sentimentality, instead of the centre of our being, the heart of the matter. Perhaps, instead, it would be better to let our minds rest on the word 'pour'. For the love which is described in the Bible, both in the Old Testament and in the New, has a strength, a generosity, an infinity about it which far transcends feeling, 'When Israel was a boy I loved him', says Hosea, not with the sentimentality of those who see children from afar, but with the realism of a parent, 'It was I who taught Ephraim to walk.' Even though they are bent on rebellion, 'How can I give you up, Ephraim, How surrender you Israel?' It is the anguished cry of a parent who has been wronged over and over again and yet cannot stop loving.

It is this same sense of the pouring out of the self for the other which informs the famous passage from I Corinthians. 'There is no limit to its faith, its hope, and its endurance. Love will never come to an end'. Anxious lovers desperately ask from their partners, 'Will you love me always?' Partners, glancing nervously at their fickleness or the waning attractions of the loved one, settle hastily for the present moment and answer reassuringly but not always quite confidently, 'Of course I will'. That is because, unless human love is rooted in God's nature as outpouring creator, it is always looking nervously over its shoulder wondering whether its strength will hold out.

That is perhaps why one of the gospels (Matthew 18:21-end) does not at first sight seem to be about love at all, but about forgiveness. As in all his teaching, Jesus gives his followers a new commandment not to follow the precepts of the law but to reflect in their lives the nature of God: 'There must be no limit to your goodness, as your heavenly Father's goodness knows no bounds' (Matthew 5:48). Forgiveness, as in the story of the prodigal son, is a good example of the practical outpouring of love. It cannot be measured out in small doses, but poured out. There is nothing sentimental about it. It is painful and costly and flows from a being who gives and gives. In human terms that can sound (and often be) either daunting or grim. Without that quality of being poured out for the sake of others the angel-tongued can create suspicion, the clever can be bullying and domineering, those with a very strong faith (and we have all met them) act as if they are superior and holier than thou, and the martyrs give the impression of seeking their own suffering. Paul's description of love seems humanly impossible, and so does going on forgiving time and time again. What Paul and Jesus are doing is to give us a glimpse of the God who shares his life with us.

Eighth Sunday
after Pentecost

The Fruit of the Spirit

Michael Townsend

FROM time to time, Church leaders make statements suggesting that if we all kept God's laws there would be no more burglary, violence, rape, AIDS, or whatever is the burning issue of the moment. If it happens to be what newspaper people call a 'slow day' when little of significance is happening, the newspapers may find room to report these statements. What, we may wonder, do Mr, Mrs and Miss Average Reader make of them? Assuming that they bother to read further than the headline as they munch their toast and marmalade, might they not recognise this as an uncontroversial, not to say self-evident statement? We can all readily agree that if everyone obeyed say, the eighth commandment, there would be an end to burglaries. Provided that Mr, Mrs or Miss Average Reader did not happen to be burglars by profession, they could presumably continue to eat their toast and marmalade and agree that the world would indeed be a better place if we all kept God's laws. The problem is that such bland statements do not seem to help very much in reducing the incidence of regrettable behaviour. As St. Paul knew very well, being aware of those things you ought not to do is not very much help if you still cannot stop doing them (Romans 7:14-24).

At a particularly troubled, yet potentially creative period in the history of God's chosen people, the prophet Ezekiel pointed to the need for a radical change in human personality. Heart and spirit, the innermost nature of a human being, required renewal and replacement (Ezekiel 36:26). Such creative activity can only be looked for from God, of course, and Ezekiel was bold enough to declare in the name of the Lord that by his grace such a thing was possible.

St. Paul, aware of his own experience that keeping the rules did not renew the human heart, contrasted two ways of life (Galatians 5:16-25). On the one hand, sexual vice, impurity, rivalry, jealousy, quarrels, factions, malice, drunkenness and orgies. On the other hand, love, joy, peace, patience, kindness, goodness, trustfulness, gentleness and self-control. There is little doubt which way of life is preferable! But is there really some way of moving from one to the other? Paul thought there was, and the key to it lies in the phrase with which he introduces his list of Christian qualities: '... the fruit of the Spirit is ...' (Galatians 5:22). We may note the singular — it is *fruit*, not *fruits*. All these together make up a Christian character, and are the work of the one Spirit of God in human lives. It is a matter, first and foremost, of letting God's Spirit dwell in us and work through us. Of course, it is important, when we are clear what God's law is, to live in the light of it. But that is not where Christian life begins and ends. When we fail to recognise this we produce neurotic, guilt-ridden Christians, who cannot live with failure — their own or that of others.

Jesus used similar language about the need to dwell in him (John 15:14), and one of today's Gospels (John 15:16-end) speaks about fruit-bearing. This is seen primarily in terms of faithfulness under persecution (John 15:20-21) and testimony to the truth of the gospel (John 15:26-27). For most Christians today, the best way of offering such testimony is by letting the world see lives surrendered to, and directed by, the Spirit of God. He alone makes things new — even the human heart!

Ninth Sunday
after Pentecost

The Whole Armour of God

Neville Clark

I must confess to being not a little thankful that, in the chorus of scriptural voices chosen to sound together, Paul finds a ranking place alongside David and great David's greater Son. Otherwise it might all have emerged as a little too easy and effortless. Indeed, I can almost hear the verdict now: 'Spiritual armoury is what counts. Goliath had his superiority in weaponry, strength, maturity, and physique. Much good did it do him! Disciples had their elective status, their missionary successes, their transfiguration experience. Much good did it do them! In the one case, a single sling-shot, powered by godly faith, disposed of Goliath for keeps. In the other case, a practitioner of prayer turned the trick. What further need have we of witnesses? Deploy righteousness, faith and prayer, and you are on a certain winner.'

The only trouble is that history and individual living are overflowing with instances of where the big battalions win out, the weakest go to the wall, faith has its nose rubbed in the dirt, and prayer registers zero result. That's why I welcome Paul, with his catalogue of contraries and his weird and wonderful credentials (2 Corinthians 6:3-10). He seems to be intent on redefining armoury by way of redefining victory. Suppose we shadow him, and see where the trail leads.

It is a high-sounding list of resources that the stormy apostle tables. Purity, knowledge, forbearance, kindness, the Holy Spirit, genuine love, truthful speech — not to mention righteousness in both hands. Even to begin to amass that kind of loot might stretch most of us to breaking point. But leave that aside! This is certainly a spiritual armoury; and you do not pick it up on the cheap. Yet it is just here that a blind alley beckons. So tempting to conclude that divine resources come in as a makeweight when, on the human level, we are outgunned. Goliath may have his massive sword and shield and helmet, but throwing godly faith into the scale occupied by Davidic sling and stone more than evens up the odds — and the giant takes a nosedive (1 Samuel 17:37-50). Believing prayer, allied to the healer's authority, matches spirit-possession pound for pound — and a lad in convulsions is liberated (Mark 9:14-29). A good dose of purity, righteousness, truth and genuine love overwhelms discordant opposition at Corinth — and Paul marches on his triumphant way. Only he doesn't!

Oh, yes. There are victories to be won. But they are strange victories. And to the naked eye they sometimes look more like defeats. Paul, with his catalogue of contraries, insists that we stubbornly hold two things together. Deploy the resources that God supplies and you may expect that giants will be toppled and healing life deal destructive chaos a slap in the face. God's battles are indeed fought not amid cloudy visions on transfiguration mountains but on common soil where human passions contend. *But* the place of victory will often look and be strangely like a cross, and the shape of victory oddly like our conventional portraits of weakness. 'As dying, and behold we live.'

Tenth Sunday after Pentecost

The Mind of Christ

Gordon Mursell

WHAT does it mean to have 'the mind of Christ'? In his letter to the Philippians, St. Paul makes it clear that it means sharing his ministry of service — 'assuming the nature of a slave.' Few of us, if we're honest, are likely to find that attractive. We're much better at consuming than caring; and even saving people sounds more exciting than serving them.

But the ministry of service which Christ incarnated and taught is neither as dull nor as obvious as it seems. First of all, it means knowing how to receive. Christian service is not at all the same as 'doing good'. Before St. Peter could be an effective disciple, he had to receive Christ's service (John 13:1-15); and even Jesus, at dinner in the Pharisee's house, knew how important it was to receive the loving service offered by the woman who anointed him (Luke 7:36-end). Before we rush out to serve others, we have to recognise our own deep inner need to receive; and sometimes we find it much much easier to busy ourselves in giving to others rather than in disposing ourselves to receive from them.

The second point about Christian service is that there is nothing remotely utilitarian about it. To have 'the mind of Christ' does not simply mean to have a bias to the poor. It means that we are to have a bias to the most apparently useless and redundant people, however unfashionable or unpopular that makes us appear. There is an appalling extravagance about the woman wasting all that precious ointment on Christ's feet. But it is no more appalling, or extravagant, than the attention Christ pays to the woman with the haemorrhage, or to Simon the Pharisee, or for that matter to Judas Iscariot, whose feet he washed. Christian service should have at its heart precisely this instinctive bias in favour of those least likely or able to respond — the dying, the apparently unproductive, the very old or the very young; and such service is judged not by its efficiency or immediate results but by the quality of love that informs it.

The third point about Christian service is the most important of all; and again the anonymous woman who anoints Christ shows us what it is. Christian service is not service of others for Christ's sake. It is service of Christ for others' sake. We serve Christ in them. So humility, the primary disposition of those who seek the mind of Christ, is not grovelling self-abasement. It is something much deeper: the capacity to discern the presence of Christ in those we serve, and particularly (as Christ had to do in serving Simon and Judas) in those most likely to hurt or disparage us. That will never be easy or popular. Yet that is precisely what having the mind of Christ entails; and it requires little effort to recognise that nothing else, and certainly nothing less, will break down barriers, or change our world.

Eleventh Sunday
after Pentecost

The Serving Community

John Cole

CHURCHES have an unfortunate habit of latching on to concepts just as they are going out of date. The image of 'the Servant Church' was all the rage just when domestic servants were almost extinct. Since then we have been sold on the image of the Church 'family' at a time when so much family life is fragile if not fragmented. The obvious image for the 1990s — to see the Church as a community of 'friends' (as Quakers have done for centuries) — is itself under threat as the principle of market forces, i.e. 'the Devil take the hindmost', bites deep into the nation's soul.

Today's scripture readings take seriously the notion of 'the serving community' but, like every image, it only points to part of the truth. We are not called blindly to serve. Jesus is quoted as saying, 'I do not call you servants any longer, because a servant does not know what his master is doing. Instead I call you friends . . .'

So it is in a spirit of friendship that we are called to serve, a friendship made possible because God has befriended us in Jesus Christ. 'All this is done by God,' wrote St. Paul, 'who through Christ changed us from enemies into his friends and give us the task of making others his friends also.'

But once we dig into what this 'serving' is all about, we discover — from no less than three of today's readings — that it cannot be separated from *suffering*.

The prophet in exile in Babylon, who wrote what we know as Isaiah 40-66, had two main images of the 'Servant':

In Chapter 42 God's servant is someone who brings justice; but he does so gently without attempting to dominate. He serves God in order to set people free and to bring them light. No patronising do-goodery here, no charitable largesse, no expecting a reward as of right for our hard work (remember the labourers in the vineyard?).

In Chapter 52 & 53, the servant only brings hope to others by losing all hope himself. Despised, tortured and killed, and yet it is by his scourging that we are healed. We tend to underestimate the cost of serving others in a selfless way — but could it be the only way we can be sure of knowing the love of God?

St. Paul was frank about linking knowing the love of God with the cost of being a disciple. 'It is not ourselves we proclaim;' he writes, 'We proclaim Jesus as Lord and ourselves as your servants for Jesus' sake.' (2 Corinthians 4:1-10)

In all this there should be no surprises — not when we look at Jesus. Those who do not understand God's love may ridicule us or try to take advantage of us. But Jesus lives out this pattern of selfless, suffering service of others and is vindicated. Cross and resurrection are both convincing and convicting. The way of the cross is proved to be God's way to life, but how many of us dare follow it?

By Jesus' time the Jews had learned to sum up their law in two commandments about love: love God and love your neighbour as yourself. Jesus endorses these but takes them deeper. Serving is an expression of loving; and Jesus' new commandment is 'Love one another *as I have loved you*.' (John 13:31-35)

Whether we prefer to see our Christian calling in terms of 'servant', 'family' or 'friend', the heart of it is Christ-like love, love enabled by God himself: 'By this love you have for one another, everyone will know that you are my disciples.'

Twelfth Sunday after Pentecost

The Witnessing Community

Peter Hall

TODAY'S readings for Year 1 in the Eucharist form a sharp scriptural commentary on the two great commandments. The lawyer correctly told Jesus that they were the key to participating in eternal life (Luke 10:25-37). From the easy generality of the two commandments, loving God and loving neighbour, we are robbed of all possibility of smug response by passages which uncompromisingly apply them in particular cases.

In Leviticus 19:9-18, we are given a string of examples of weak neighbours who can always be ignored without redress: the strangers who are to be allowed to pick up the remnants of the harvest; or the deaf, who are not to be treated with contempt; or the hired person who has no power to demand wages for work already done, if the employer chooses to wait until tomorrow, or the end of the week. The shifting sands of human life meant that the people of Israel, who had once themselves been aliens, and slaves with no power to demand justice, were now land owners. God required of them never to forget their Egypt experience. His unshifting nature, 'I am the Lord', meant that he called his people Israel to behave in exactly the same ways of justice which he had demanded of the Egyptians, and they had ignored.

When the lawyer gave his response to Jesus in the passage from Luke he also wanted concrete examples of what is a neighbour. He could not have known at the time he asked the question that for once the two commandments were one. The person facing him merged the two commandments in a unique way. The followers of Jesus Christ eventually perceived that to love him was to love a weak neighbour, one who had no redress if he was treated with contempt, one against whom people nursed hatred, and against whom they took sides on a capital charge. He was also God, — to be loved with heart, soul, strength and mind.

People could no longer make the distinction that John makes in his epistle — it is so much eaier to say we love an invisible God than a visible neighbour (1 John 4:15-end). The two were one: to love my neighbour Jesus is to love the Lord my God. But of course he was not loved. The spirit of merciful justice that pervades Leviticus 19 was never shown to the one who combined the two great commandments in himself. In the name of loving God, God who had covenanted to become a weak neighbour was made the object of our hatred.

The embarrassing thing about Jesus is that he removes our usual excuse for not loving our neighbour, i.e., that our neighbour is unlovable. By grim duty we might succeed part of the time in loving those who are not lovable, but at least we have the defence that it is such a difficult task. Surely Jesus was (in theory) the most lovable neighbour there has ever been, so it should have been easy. If not, why not? It could just be that the real problem about loving God and neighbour lies within ourselves. Of course there are plenty of unlovable neighbours around, including ourselves, but the starkness of the situation that the lawyer faced (unknowingly) was that he was spelling out the two commandments to this most lovable of all neighbours. Oddly enough, Jesus' story about the Good Samaritan did not answer his question about defining the neighbour. Instead it promised the lawyer that he could be as free as the Samaritan to be a neighbour. His final words of command are almost a promise: 'Go, you have the humanity in you to do the same as the Samaritan, even though you are so tied to your religious tradition, even though you have just set out to put me to the test, rather than being a neighbour to me.'

Paul's passage on love in Romans (12:9ff) runs through to 13:10. At first it seems to be full of generalities, but then suddenly homes-in in the same concrete way on the issue of vengeance. It raises for us not just a question of the weak neighbour, or the neighbour who is also God, but the neighbour who hurts us. What we want instinctively to do about such a neighbour is to take vengeance. Being a neighbour to someone who hurts us can mean forgiveness, but surely it is God who is good at forgiving rather than us. Why not then do the thing we find much easier, to take vengeance, and ask God to do the forgiving? The reply is thunderous: you are to do the forgiving, 'I will repay, says the Lord'. We are not safe to be let loose on vengeance, but we are to be neighbours by forgiving. We are to be neighbours particularly to those who have no redress, and forgive them for the demands that they make upon us. We are to be neighbour to the one who once turned out to be God. Even he needs our forgiveness, — for not being what we would try to make him — especially when he is insistently present again today, — in those listed in Leviticus 19, or in Jesus' parable of the sheep and the goats.

Thirteenth Sunday after Pentecost

~

The Suffering Community

Robert Williamson

THE Philippian Christians were graced with two blessings. They were given the twin gifts of believing and suffering. To believe in Christ and to suffer for him is part of the calling of the Christian community. Any objective survey of both the Old and New Testaments would leave us in little doubt that if we have a passion to see right prevail, and if we are prepared to stand up for the truth of the Gospel, then suffering in some shape or form is only to be expected. Even the Servant of the Lord in Isaiah, despite his daily attentiveness to the will of God, and his apt use of the word of God to sustain the weary, was on the receiving end of undeserved suffering (Isaiah 50:4-9a). An experience that was to be paralleled in somewhat sharper focus in the life of our Lord — the ideal Servant. For him also, the doing of God's will provoked conflict, and the apt word was not always acceptable — even within his local congregation!

The intimate connection between believing and suffering can all too easily be dismissed as a combination belonging to a past age. Even if we reluctantly admit that it is part of today's world, it tends to be quickly and conveniently assigned to those countries such as South Africa which are distanced from us. But the matter cannot be so lightly set aside. Those who take their stand with Christ, as a necessary consequence put themselves on a collision course with all that is hostile to the Gospel and, as night follows day, so suffering is inevitable.

Very often today's suffering, like today's society, is rather more sophisticated than in Stephen's day (Acts 7:54-8:1). To challenge the prejudices of our society in the name of Christ will normally bring not stones but ridicule, and to dare to challenge the prejudices of the Church is likely to be met with the self-righteous charge of 'knocking a hole in the bottom of the boat'. Jeremiah's experience is not unique (Jeremiah 20:7-11a); the Church has as little regard for prophets today as it ever had.

However, for suffering to be redemptive it must surely be undeserved, the result of faith rather than of folly. The stand taken by Stephen and the Church in Jerusalem resulted in persecution and death, but it was the commitment of *faith*, and though the Church was scattered, the Gospel was spread. A Church which is insensitive in its proclamation, impractical in its exhortation and lacking integrity in its life, deserves to have its witness ridiculed and its gospel ignored. But it must accept the blame for its folly, rather than fantasize about the opposition it encounters claiming it to be undeserved suffering for the sake of Christ.

We need no reminding of course, that suffering for the sake of Christ can be so easily avoided. The unsavoury secret is to keep silent when gospel principles are being flouted, and to acquiesce in things like racism or social injustice. The desire for a quiet life is not unusual, but it is seldom realised for those who are called and sent to be 'like sheep in the midst of wolves'.

The cross is the model of redemptive suffering. It is also to be the hallmark of the Church. The proof of Jesus's identity were the scars he bore, and because of them his disciples believed (John 20:21). A Church which does not bear the scars and wounds of suffering love will lack credibility in its ministry to a suffering world. How can we speak of a God who will one day wipe away all tears and not begin to dry the tears and heal the wounds of those who suffer and are oppressed now?

Finally, as the gospel reading from John reminds us (John 16:1-11), the cross and the Gospel have a word of judgement as well as a word of reconciliation for the world. The values taught by Christ are in stark contrast to those so often practised in the world and we need to witness to them over against the world. The Church is not called to preserve its own life but to follow the example of the one who gave his life as a ransom for many. He followed the way of suffering which was revealed as the way of glory. This is the way that the Master trod, shall not his servants tread it still?

Fourteenth Sunday
after Pentecost

The Family

Rodney Matthews

THE model of the family is extraordinarily resilient. Despite depressing statistics of broken marriages and 'single-parent' families, alarming reports of violence and abuse within close-knit relationships, and personal experiences which bring the vulnerability of the family too close to home for comfort, the concept of the family as the base unit of society persists.

The classic picture of father, mother, son and daughter remains the norm from which spring many variations and extensions. Curiously, the stability of the family does not seem to depend upon roles perfectly performed, however desirable it is to be faithful. Human failure is not sufficient to destroy the ideal pattern.

The Bible relates numerous such stories, and many concern soured relationships: from Cain and Abel, Joseph and his brothers, through to the woman of Samaria who seemed unable to sustain any marriage bond for long. In addition to moving personal accounts there is a consistent call for qualities that help to ensure a stability of the family. Three of today's readings have a single constant thread: *fidelity*.

Here is a quality much under-rated today in a world of conditional values, bargaining and tit-for-tat reprisals that attempt to build upon the shaky foundation of rights and counter-claims, instead of upon the sacrifice of constant self-giving. Proverbs 31:10-31 may not prove the most popular of images in a society of equal rights, but it is an authentic example of fulfilment through faithfulness. Paul takes up the same theme of loyalty to commitment and demonstrates, (Ephesians 5:25-6:4), that it should flow through the whole family and is not dependent upon reciprocal responses. And when Jesus was challenged about the possible breakdown of marriage, (Mark 10:2-16), the stand he took was unequivocally about truth in relationships, which he then demonstrated in a delightful cameo portrait of his unaffected reception of children.

Throughout the bible the pattern is clear and uncompromising. The Christian model of the family can withstand any strains or threats because at its heart is singular resolution to duty: and it is a model for community itself, at whatever level. All the time there is constancy, even of one party only — as in the classic story of Hosea's relationship to Gomer, or the father's stand in the story of the Prodigal Son — there is security. It is this faithfulness to the ideal that augers well for society, in spite of the shocks of failure that are invariably demonstrations of the destructiveness of self-acclaim or selfish desire. The idea of the family is popular because ultimately it offers peace, protection and fulfilment. It is a goal that is achievable, although not without effort. The success rate is less important than the target, and the reward of self-giving, whatever the cost, infinitely outweighs the sacrifice. That is the gospel.

Fifteenth Sunday
after Pentecost

Those in Authority

Neville Clark

THREE contrasting lectionary tableaux confront our wondering gaze. On the left is King Solomon on one of his good days. On the right is King Herod on one of his bad days. In the centre is a somewhat indistinct portrait of a Roman King-Emperor and sundry acolytes. What are we to make of them?

Clearly, Solomon is the good guy. He is much in church. He is probably a believer in the Divine Right of Kings. Certainly he stands as God's appointee with leadership responsibilities for God's chosen nation. With proper humility he seeks the wise discerning mind essential for the discharge of such heavy responsibility. We are not surprised that he is awarded bonus points (1 Kings 3:4-15).

Equally clearly, Herod is the bad guy. He is much in his palace. His forte is the unmentionable. He probably believes in the Divine Right of Kings as well. He has a sensitive ear for any threat to his position or his reputation. He likes to please his womenfolk. Evidently and properly he will come to a sticky end (Matthew 14:1-12).

Dead centre is a first century Caesar and an indefinite mass of lesser potentates in high positions. They are not represented as doing anything very much. The hope seems to be that they will leave lesser mortals alone. It may be salutary to offer a prayer to that effect. (1 Timothy 2:1-7)

So where does that leave us? It's a bit like a tour round an ancient portrait gallery. Interesting things to be seen. Some fine brushwork here and there. All a bit remote. Now back to the modern city, democracy, the ballot box, the party political broadcast, and the latest town hall scandal.

Of course, we can skim across the centuries, hopefully replace Solomon with any occupant of No 10, substitute some suitably distant potentate for ungodly Herod, let Parliament stand in for the collective centre piece, and pray wisdom for one and all. Perhaps, on the whole, that is what we do. And if sometimes the imagination boggles, we may rightly remind ourselves that everyone needs prayer and that, in our unstable world, leaders may require a double portion.

Only it may be that, from time to time, we might add two postscripts to these self-evident conclusions. Back of those seamy or improving portraits is the wider broader biblical canvas of a world in which authority is delegated authority, accountable to the God who has loaned it out for a season. Once authority ceases to be held as a trust it is replaced by naked power, unrestrained because unaccountable. In turn, there follows the sobering realisation that few there be who are not somewhere, somehow, wielders of authority. From the most revered of legislators to the humblest of parents the entrustment of authority runs, that the fabric of human society may survive. That we are all 'in high positions' makes the sweep of authority, the scope of responsibility, and the urgent need for wisdom and discernment, universal. In the end, to pray for those in authority is to pray for ourselves.

Sixteenth Sunday
after Pentecost

The Neighbour

John Cole

THE best known neighbours in the British Isles today are surely those who live in Ramsey Street, Australia. There the residents totter from one complex situation to the next, from crisis to crisis, all to retain the devotion of millions of soap opera addicts.

In the real world back home, surprisingly few people manage much contact with their neighbours at all — beyond complaining when one interferes with the other's privacy! In many villages residents have no reason to walk down the street, except perhaps to walk the dog or post a letter. For everything else they travel by car. Result: they hardly ever see the neighbours to speak to them. In suburban areas the same is often true, especially when houses change hands frequently. Many will admit that they don't even know the names of the people next door. That's how far community life has declined in this land.

All this has a very strange and dangerous consequence, and church people are not immune. Apart from in our place of work, we are now in a situation where we do not have to talk to anyone unless we choose to, and that usually means talking only to people we find agreeable, who look at life in much the same way as we do. The danger, of course, is that this reinforces prejudice, for how can we understand why other people think differently if we never meet them?

Gatherings of the like-minded can be virtually all that is left of 'community' in some places. But when people meet only because they like each other's company, this is a standing denial of neighbourliness or a real community spirit. How many local churches fall into this trap — a self-centred club built round the preferences of the congregation? The gospel of market forces and consumer choice says there is nothing wrong with this; the command to love your neighbour and the Christian Gospel of God's love for all say something very different.

124

The whole point of loving our neighbour is that our neighbour is probably not someone we like very much. The very fact that he is our neighbour almost guarantees there will be something which irritates us!

Jesus' story of the Good Samaritan (Luke 10:25-37) hits the nail on the head but is usually misunderstood. It is not telling us to be kind to anyone in need. Most of us can manage that if the need is obvious enough; and afterwards it is rather nice to sit back and polish our haloes. The logic of the Good Samaritan story is much more humbling and more demanding in the long run: it is telling us to appreciate the unselfish generosity and kindness of those we would normally mistrust or despise.

Loving our neighbour, therefore, is really about appreciating all those people we don't really like. And even though the Old Testament command is 'Love your neighbour *as yourself*' (Leviticus 19:18), we ought not to be surprised; for we don't really like ourselves all that much at times!

Three final thoughts:

1. The 'Holiness Code' in Leviticus (one of today's Old Testament readings) was a wonderful idea but it never worked. You can't legislate to make people unselfish.

2. The early Christians were a motley crowd, an unruly mixture of classes, cultures, languages and religious backgrounds; but one thing impressed pagans more than anything else. 'See,' they said, 'how these Christians love one another!'

3. Humbly appreciating someone else's generosity is a pretty good description of what loving *God* is all about as well. As St. John put it, 'We are to love, then, because He first loved us.' (1 John 4:19).

Seventeenth Sunday
after Pentecost

The Proof of Faith

Rodney Matthews

'THE proof of the pudding is in the eating'. The ingredients may seem of excellent quality; the recipe may read as an ingenious concoction and imaginative blending; the reputation of the chef may be witnessed by certificates of his *haute cuisine:* but the pudding will be judged by the palate. So with faith.

What is demonstrated by deeds is, of course, derived. 'Every good and perfect gift comes from above' (James 1:16). We start off with perfect ingredients. We are given a classic recipe, sometimes with contemporary variations. We may have learned the theory and got a certificate of faith, a written declaration of 'a Christian'. The test is still to come. Principles can only be judged by practice, and practice betrays the grasp of first principles.

When Jeremiah (7:1-11) spoke out against the false prophets of his day his charge was that their chant was hollow, derived from errors somewhere down the line. 'The temple of the Lord' had developed into an empty catch-phrase, a superstitious calling up of a myth that a sacred building is bound to offer security. Jeremiah started at the other end. He sampled the behaviour around him and didn't like the taste. Theft, murder, adultery, perjury, idolatry — his experienced palate traced in the corrupt mixture the basis for a disaster. There was no hiding the poison however it was dressed up.

James (1:16-end) used his own metaphor for the faith/works connection, and it is a teasing one. Look in a mirror and what do you see? The image is only as accurate as the memory to retain it. Today photography can jolt that memory but also challenge it. We may not like the photograph and protest 'I don't look like that, do I?', perhaps because we remembered ourselves as better looking than we are! The point James is making is that it is the faith that is borne out in action which is the reality of what is there. Only the wishful imagination may confuse as the memory plays tricks.

We are taught to *do* what we believe we *are*. Are we grateful for the goodness of God? Then what are we doing about that state of gratitude? If the answer, like that of nine out of ten lepers (Luke 17:11-19), is 'nothing', it calls into question the sincerity of appreciation. No amount of self justification or excuses avail. Action gives the lie to pretence.

The issue is always personal. The credentials of the Christian are tested by the manner of his life day by day, and each day's offering is only as good as it is tested to be. This, however, is not justification by works but is the reality of justification by faith. For faith is no illusionist's trick with baptism or absolution camouflaging the bad that is actually there by giving it an appearance of goodness. It is rather the miracle of a life surrendered to the Christ who redeems God's good gift and sets it free to manifest itself in responsive action. Real faith proves itself in action.

Eighteenth Sunday
after Pentecost

The Offering of Life

Peter Hall

GENEROSITY is the keynote of the Christian perception of God's love. In Jesus Christ, God shows himself as generous to the point of recklessness, bursting all our human calculations on what can be wisely and prudently promised and hoped for.

Nehemiah 6:1-16 is part of a book which, throughout its length, has delightful flashes of the personality of Nehemiah. From the beginning in the court of the Persian Emperor, he repeatedly takes risky steps and prays desperately that all might succeed. He gets to Jerusalem, and rebuilds the walls in the face of stiff opposition from without, as in chapter 6, and from within, as the plight of the poor creates havoc in the small Jewish community. His political position was very precarious, and repeated messages back to the Persian court could quickly rob him of his governorship. It is not sure even now that it was good to build the walls. Ironically, by chapter 11, people were chosen to live in the city by drawing lots, and anybody who volunteered was greatly admired.

As we read the whole story, what stands out and challenges us is the generous and reckless faith of Nehemiah, responding to God whom he believed wanted his people back in Jerusalem and Judah. 'Should a man like me run away?'. Surrounded by enemies who might attack, or get him removed as governor, he would not hear the prudent advice of those who said they wanted to protect him. He perceived it as 'frightening me into compliance and into committing sin' — sin was anything less than total commitment to building the walls day by day, fully armed, without even time to take off clothes at night. The generosity of Nehemiah's response to God expressed itself in a similar generosity towards people, taking none of the special 'perks' that a governor could take, and feeding hundreds of people regularly at his table.

The words of the author of the first letter of Peter (1 Peter

4:7-11) seem at first sight to have a very different and cautious spirit, 'ordered and sober'. In fact it is about being ordered and sober in the face of the possibility that every new day might widen out into eternity, — 'the end'. It is not the prudential soberness that plans for this life as though it is going to be for ever, and saves and protects itself. It is about keeping cool and watchful and praying, in the face of a world that panics because it does not understand the seeds of its own destruction. Christians are to get excited about how to build up each other in love — a love which in its forgiveness, generosity and willingness to suffer, openness to more hurt, to give people time, sweeps away 'innumerable sins'. Opening our homes to each other in an ungrudging, unfussy way is an immediate practical sign of that generosity. Using the gifts that we have been given in order to build each other up, rather than protecting ourselves, is a generous life-style that, in a day which might open up into eternity, will find itself entirely affirmed.

Jesus' parable of the talents, (Matthew 25:14-30) is like many of his stories, a winkling out of those things that already lie in our hearts. It is a story about a generous master, who was perceived as being 'a hard man'. Where did the picture of his master, described by the man with one talent, come from? Jesus instinctively picked it out from the hearts and minds of those around him, and it is a picture about God. At the bottom of our hearts we suspect he is 'a hard man', reaping where he has not sown and gathering where he has not scattered. So we have to be careful, and take steps to ensure that we have some rights that we can claim when we come before him: 'Here it is, it was yours, you have it back.' — no room for complaint! Nothing could be further from the reckless generosity of God that is revealed in Jesus Christ. Nothing could be further from the generosity of the man in the parable, who wants his servants to 'come and join in your master's happiness'.

This story probes into an elusive mystery about our own hearts. Why is it, in the face of a God who is so recklessly generous in his creation, and even more so in his redemptive work in Jesus Christ, that we still have a deep instinct which tells us not to trust such a generosity, and that the reality behind it is 'a hard man'? It is a very understandable feeling for those whose experience of human beings is one of continual hardness, and whose conditions of life have been unremittingly miserable. But the 'hard man' lurks in all our hearts, no matter how pleasant the circumstances of our lives and generous the provision that has been made. Often the more generous the provision we have experienced, the deeper the desire to control it, to keep it, and to even increase it.

The other two servants took risks with what they had been given, and Nehemiah-like, the risks paid off. They found themselves with the promise of entering their master's happiness. Also Nehemiah-like, it did not mean that they were necessarily wise, and always made the right decision in the risks they took. What mattered was that in response to a tremendous generosity, they in turn were prepared to take risks in the same generous spirit — not assuming they were dealing with a hard man, but one who would understand if it all went wrong. Live every day, says Peter, reflecting that reckless generosity of love to each other, because today may be the day when all of us enter the happiness that our master wants to share, and all things are fulfilled.

Nineteenth Sunday
after Pentecost

The Life of Faith

Timothy Jenkins

JACOB, who was a wily man, wanted, if not proof, good evidence for faith, grounds upon which he could believe. What sort of evidence for faith is available to us?

We can look in two directions. The first is, that in our dealings with things and people we are from time to time surprised. Matters and situations pose their own questions, truth has its own demands, and we cannot entirely control or anticipate these questions and demands, but must simply follow where they lead. We cannot know in advance, even about ourselves. Reality — or the world — is open-ended; it is not clear what it would mean to know all about it.

The second direction is somewhat contradictory to the first, for it seems possible to compare things and to make sense; in other words, there is some evidence that things fit together, that they belong in some way to a larger pattern, even if it is not possible to say overall what that pattern is or what it will come to or look like.

In Christian belief, these 'evidences' are both aspects of Jesus Christ. On the one hand, because God's life has been lived in the limits and forms imposed by matter and history, in the life of a man, there is no possibility of summing up the potential of matter and history, even of our lives, and of knowing it in advance. There is always more to life than can be known; we might call this an 'excess of possibility'.

On the other hand, because this 'excess' arises out of Jesus Christ, the presence of God in our midst, these possibilities do not simply multiply endlessly and without meaning, but rather point to the fact that in the end everything will make sense in Jesus Christ. He is the 'coming home', or the key, to all the trajectories contained in this excess of possibility.

The two sorts of 'evidence' help to give a shape to the life of faith. First, you cannot live by knowledge alone, with absolute control and guarantees, but only with an awareness of the openness of things, and of the impossibility of having everything sewn up. Indeed, the desire to have complete control is a fantasy and a retreat from engaging with things as they are. Second, there is no need to despair, for there are always glimpses of the possibility that things will make sense, that there is some sort of purpose and shape and, indeed, warmth to things.

The life of faith is then to do with recognizing the realities that lie outside oneself and responding to them, using them as resources and in so doing, becoming evidence for faith. The passage from Matthew (6:24-end) discusses at a mundane level the double business of first realizing that most of what is important goes on outside one's control, and second of finding resources in the final purpose to which all this activity points. The verses from Hebrews (11:1-2 & 8-16) are more exalted in tone, and point to famous examples of faith, to people who relied upon God and who have thereby become evidence of his power and purpose.

This is, in brief, the life of faith: to seek resources outside oneself (through prayer and perseverance), and through that seeking to become evidence for faith.

Twentieth Sunday
after Pentecost

Endurance

John Cole

WAITING is not a popular pastime. Advertisers made good use of this fact of human nature when they introduced us to our Flexible Friend who 'takes the waiting out of wanting'.

Yet there is nothing unhealthy about waiting. In fact increasing numbers of people in service industries in Britain are doing it all the time as a profession. They are waiters and waitresses; for there is less difference between the notions of waiting *for* things and waiting *on* people than we generally suppose.

A good waiter is attentive but doesn't interfere with those he is serving until the time is right. Christians are in business waiting on God until the time is right for him when, in St. Paul's words in one of today's readings, 'the creation itself will be set free from its bondage to decay and obtain the glorious liberty of the children of God' (Romans 8:18-25).

Of course, waiting is hard work. It is not just 'hanging about' and doing nothing. It is painful, frustrating, unavoidable — but creative, like the pain (to use St. Paul's analogy) of giving birth.

It is always much easier to give up waiting, to give up being attentive to God and go off to please ourselves — or even to go off to please others. Three faithful Jews in the court of Nebuchadnezzar — so that marvellous story goes — ended up in the blazing furnace because they would not give up their loyalty to God, because they would not defer to the king's wishes; and a Christ-figure was seen with them as they walked unharmed in the fire (Daniel 3:13-26).

But why should we complain? God surely has a much more frustrating time than we do, waiting on us! He attends to our every need moment by moment and gets precious little thanks! All the while he is waiting for us to turn and acknowledge his love.

In one of the Gospel readings, the disciples wanted divine retribution to fall on a Samaritan village because it would not agree to a visit from Jesus; but Jesus ticks them off (Luke 9:51-end). We would be in a sorry state if God did not wait to pass judgement!

But this is not the end of the story. The disciples were impatient and that was wrong; but Jesus points them to the positive alternative course of action. 'Never mind about anything else', he says in effect; 'you just follow me'. St. John, at the end of his Gospel, recalled a similar message in a completely different context: 'Never mind about what may happen to the beloved disciple', the risen Christ tells Peter; 'You just follow me.' (John 21:20-22)

Following Jesus, understanding and living out the pattern of unselfish love that he expressed in his life and death, is the hard but fruitful road to life and liberty for the children of God. It is a piece of selfless self-discipline — no masochism here, no fanaticism, not even 'endurance' (despite the use of this word for the Sunday theme) for this suggests too rigid and passive a role — but rather a quiet single-minded attentiveness (like a good waiter) which makes complete sense because it is focussed unshakeably on God whose victory is assured.

Twenty-First Sunday
after Pentecost

The Christian Hope

John Cole

A clarion call sounds from today's readings: our hope is secure, for Christ is risen. It is the climax of three sets of readings affirming that God is God of the future who has given us himself in the here and now.

Two weeks ago the emphasis was on the need to walk by faith and not to be anxious. Last week we learned single-mindedness — the ability to cope with frustration and the discipline of following in the way of Christ.

This week the promise is: God's Kingdom is not as delayed as you think; don't lose heart in your praying; God's justice is being done and done speedily; for in a very real sense our hope is fulfilled already — for Christ is risen.

One of the most thrilling things about the Scriptures is their forward-looking quality. It is as though God is located beyond our horizon into the future, yet chooses to make himself known in our own lives. The light from over the horizon was glimpsed by the prophets of the Old Testament and found dynamic expression in the continuing and 'saving' relationship God had with his ancient people the Jews; and it culminated in God's final self-revelation and presence in the life, death and resurrection of Jesus of Nazareth.

Habakkuk was not the most outstanding of those ancient prophets, but in one of today's readings he speaks confidently of God who will not delay in fulfilling his promises — and the particular promise is this: life for those who are faithful to God (Habakkuk 2:1-4).

Ezekiel, always out to shock his hearers, echoes in another passage set for today the notion of 'no delay'. '"Even as I speak, it shall be done." This is the very word of the Lord.' (Ezekiel 12:21-end) And noticeably God makes this promise out of annoyance with his 'rebellious people' who have got so depressed that they have projected any thought of a God who acts far into the future.

It is our own inability (or refusal) to recognise God who is already acting or has already acted, which leads so many people today to be anxious about the future. Novelists reflect the mood of a society today which one of them summed up as 'not daring to hope any more'. This is not the petty anxiety about today or tomorrow which concerned us in the readings a fortnight ago. This is the global unease that people are feeling about the way we are destroying our own planet — *God's* world — through our greed and short-sightedness.

'Humanly speaking I'm a pessimist,' Archbishop Michael Ramsey was once heard to say — and with every justification! 'Only God permits me to be an optimist.' And here in today's readings is the reason for the optimism, the confident hope: the power of God that raised Jesus from the dead and the life that is already ours in Christ.

The certainty of the resurrection (even though we cannot fully understand what that implies) has always been the cornerstone of the Christian hope. The risen Christ is the focus of St. Paul's defence before King Agrippa (Acts 26:1-8) and it is the focus where the newly-baptised readers of the first letter of Peter must put their trust (1 Peter 1:13-21). 'I am the resurrection and I am life' Jesus tells Martha after the raising of Lazarus (John 11:17-27) — but the ultimate question remains as expressed in another of today's readings: even after such assurances, 'when the Son of Man comes, will he find any faith on earth?' (Luke 18:1-8)

Coming to terms with this greater reality which we call the resurrection is not easy. In the New Testament, as earlier in Ezekiel, it emerges as a paradox: God's Kingdom is already here — but not yet; we are called to become 'through Christ' what we already are 'in Christ' (the way St. Paul uses the notions of 'through Christ' and 'in Christ' is fascinating and not always faithfully reproduced in translation).

A sense of 'already but not yet' feels remarkably appropriate for Christians in today's fast changing world. Old 'structural' notions of 'God's in his heaven; all's well with the world' are out of place. But in their place, if we have the courage, is the more dynamic New Testament gospel that in the end, and so here and now as well, 'our God reigns' — for Christ is risen!

Twenty-Second Sunday after Pentecost

The Two Ways

Neville Clark

BLACK and white are, I suppose, our favourite religious colours. Right is right and wrong is wrong. Good is good and evil is evil. What we are asked to do is to choose and act upon the choice. In its own way, it is an uncomplicated world thus presented.

How does it go? Obedience to the right promises blessing, life, success, and a good conscience into the bargain. Opting for evil will bring a thumbs down, somehow, somewhere. What could be fairer than that? Deuteronomy surely gets it starkly right (Deuteronomy 11:18-28). And the Johannine letter nicely adds a walloping Christian sanction (1 John 2:22-end). Behind right is true belief in and about Jesus the Christ. Behind the other thing are false lies and the antichrist; and you can't get more damning than that! Game, set and match to orthodoxy — the place where we dwell. Suppose we talk about something more open to discussion!

Of course, we are not entirely oblivious to the siren voices that are already objecting loudly. Cries of intolerance and prejudice shrieking all over the place. Frenzied protestations that life is not like that. Even the dawning recognition that, sometimes, among those qualifying voices may be our own. Not easy to play a straight and nerveless bat in face of all that bodyline bowling.

Suppose we brace ourselves now for the real corker. Just when we were not prepared for it, the Jesus of the Gospels is about to send down a googly! While Deuteronomy and its New Testament ally look on aghast, the Dishonest Steward makes an entrance and wins a commendation (Luke 16:1-9). That is guaranteed to despatch the finest Christian doctrinal and ethical performer back to the pavilion. Evidently it is time for a post mortem.

So what is really happening when Jesus of Nazareth strides into the complexities of human life? It means decision day. It means that a new unheralded world is crashing into the old. It means that the familiar ground is trembling. It means that a crisis has been reached. It means that life and death are in the balance. It means that decisive action is the only relevant response. Even a dishonest steward — especially a dishonest steward — has enough gumption to realise that, when zero hour strikes, he can no longer sit on his hands but must hazard all. Are those who secretly and self-admiringly lay claim to being sons of light to mudge and fudge when God is at the doors?

The secret and the difficulty is always how to recognise, amid the murky mists of our confusion, the presence of Jesus, how to distinguish truth and goodness from prejudice and self-righteousness, and how to come to terms with the exchange rate of that foreign coinage in which the Kingdom of God finally pays all debts. Discerning and choosing will always involve a hazard, made in sensitivity and humility. Yet, living with the biblical tradition and binding it as 'a sign upon your hand' will take us some way towards 'abiding in the truth' and gaining the mind-set that belongs to children of God.

Last Sunday
after Pentecost

The Citizens of Heaven

Gordon Roe

S AY the word 'city' and you are likely to produce a confusion of images nowadays. If we leave on one side the picture of economic wizardry and financial mystification presented by The City, there is the deprivation associated with Inner Cities described in the report, *Faith in the City*, which has directed our attention not just to financial questions but to a whole range of social and theological questions too. And behind them is lingering somewhere a Romantic picture of a city as a town, teeming with all sorts of interrelated interests, and at its heart a cathedral with its quiet close and transcendent beauty.

Throughout Christian history there has been the temptation to say that we can escape the miseries of the inner cities (and their equivalent in previous ages) by looking forward to life in a heavenly city after we die. 'Jerusalem the Golden with milk and honey blest', wrote St. Bernard, 'Beneath thy contemplation sink heart and voice opprest' or, more explicitly, a sixteenth century hymn-writer: 'Jerusalem my happy home, when shall I come to thee? When shall my sorrows have an end, Thy joys when shall I see?' In Ely Cathedral, the tombstone of the second Bishop, Nigel, depicts him as naked (except for his pastoral staff) being borne up into a heaven which looks like the Romanesque walled city of his day.

It is wrong to believe, though, that in some periods of Christian history it has been assumed that the only way of attaining the heavenly city is by dying. There is a strong tradition which says that we can have a foretaste of it now. After all one of today's readings (Philippians 3:7-end) says 'our household is in heaven' (or, as the *New English Bible* translates it 'We are citizens of heaven'). St. Bernard ended his ecstatic picture of that homeland, 'His only, his for ever, Thou shalt be, and *thou art*.' The Anglo-Catholics and ritualists of nineteenth century London and Leeds were helping the poor to experience heaven now, not simply promising them it hereafter.

The tension between the now and the hereafter is expressed in the reading from Philippians where St. Paul acknowledges that his life is a pilgrimage: 'I forget the past and I strain ahead for what is still to come.' And yet, to some extent he knows that he has already been given a place in Christ, he is a citizen of heaven.

Even this idea of a foretaste of heaven does not quite do justice to St. John's teaching of 'eternity now': 'Eternal life is this: to know you, the only true God and Jesus Christ whom you have sent.' That brings us back to our present responsibility and experience. As Jeremiah says, 'Seek the welfare of the city where I have sent you into exile.' Your citizenship of heaven consists not in longing to be somewhere other than where you are now, but in knowing God and his son Jesus Christ in your present situation. Our pilgrimage consists not in being *brought* to life eternal but in the constant struggle to be *kept* in it.

All Saints

The Cloud of Witnesses

Neville Clark

WHAT dispirited travellers need, I am told, is a pick-me-up, or at least the promise of an oasis round the next bend. Evidently the author of the letter to the Hebrews thought so too. All very well to promise Christian pilgrims God, both here and hereafter; but even God can have a vaguely sinister and abrasive ring, not exactly calculated to fire sagging muscles. In any event, this writer's view of the middle distance is painted in less sombre fashion (Hebrews 12:18-24). No storm clouds, thunder or lightning. Rather, something more like a family festival where God and judgement, Jesus and grace, are inextricably intertwined, where home is the venue, where elder brothers and sisters, long since arrived, make celebration, and where angelic attendants doubtless look faintly ridiculous in fancy dress. Not too far from the spiritual equivalent of champagne corks popping, we may be tempted to conclude.

The biblical artist might not take mortal offence at the comparison. He would however wish to add two qualifying riders to the conclusion. The celebration has been mounted at very considerable divine cost. There has been a price for turning an old covenant into a new, and covenanters had better be aware of it. Under the old covenant, Jerusalem's annual Day of Atonement centred on the High Priest's entry into the awful and fearful Holy of Holies, the dwelling place of God. Under the new covenant, there is open access to a Father's arms and a Father's house; but Jesus, the High Priest, gave his life to achieve it. If there is laughter, it has been bought with tears.

And thus and so, if the invitation is out broadcast to weary travellers to keep on the homeward road and eventually join the celebration, they had better take the party seriously and make sure they make pilgrimage in the right direction. The invitation cards are in fact of a curious character, as Jeremiah (31:31-34) and Matthew (5:1-12) between them hasten to make crystal clear. The new covenant has its marching orders inscribed not on Mosaic tablets of stone but in the flesh and blood of forgiven human hearts. And the dancing happiness of family celebration belongs to the poor, the mourners, the meek, the merciful, the pure, the peacemakers, the persecuted, and those whose palates are attuned to righteousness.

We call it saintliness. Really, it is all about family likeness, and very little about extraordinary piety. From one point of view, the 'saints' are indeed unusual people, exceptional because of the startling imprint of christlikeness that they bear. To give thanks for them is to celebrate heroes of faith who sweetened earth and gladden heaven. Yet equally, from another point of view, the 'saints' are all the pilgrims and covenanters in whom the image of Christ is being formed and the life of Christ is taking shape. They scent just over the brow of every hill the banquet of the Kingdom. They have no means of identification except the family resemblance. They have nothing in common, except a common name and a common home.